Praise for *Stay and Prevail: Students of Color Don't Need to Leave Their Communities to Succeed*

"Our young people of color are descendants of powerful, creative, and resilient ancestors whose contributions permeate every aspect of life. *Stay and Prevail* calls our young people to action, reminding them that they too are called to contribute to our rich legacy. Schools can be identity-affirming spaces when we are intentional."

—**Kaya Henderson,** CEO of Reconstruction, cohost of Pod Save the People, and former Chancellor of DC Public Schools

"In a world where self-improvement and academic achievement have been offered no legitimate root for the most marginalized, Gutiérrez and Padilla offer an anchoring, thorough, beautiful disruption and reanalysis. This book speaks to noble souls in subaltern spaces and reminds the world that academic success cannot be the pursuit of acceptance in worlds far from home. For a Ratchetdemic scholar from the Bronx and others like me, and for those in pursuit of understanding those like us, this work offers much needed radical possibility. A solid read!"

—**Chris Emdin,** author of Ratchetdemic: Reimagining Academic Success and STEM STEAM Make Dream

"*Stay and Prevail* is a reminder to educators that our stories open up the intimate channels of connectedness that our young people need—without having to leave our homes. I became a founding school principal in my home community because I wanted to serve students who lived like me, looked like me, and had attainable dreams, just like me. Gutiérrez and Padilla offer us the leadership antidote for actively dismantling the Leave to Succeed mindset. Their book is filled with immeasurable wisdom and countless examples of leaders who shared their journeys of pain and contribution."

—**Karen Maldonado,** EdLD, Chief Program and Innovation Officer of Latinos for Education and founding principal and executive director of leadership with the New York City Department of Education

"We don't do enough to share stories of the communities that shaped us. *Stay and Prevail* calls us to action—naming a harmful deficit-based practice and challenging us to be the change we want to see."

—**Tommy Chang**, CEO of New Teacher Center, the cohost of "miseducAsian," and former superintendent of Boston Public Schools

"I vividly recall experiencing the profoundly positive impact of the Black educators from our community who taught me and my peers. Years later, I'd follow in their footsteps and return to lead West Philadelphia classrooms and schools of my own.

So, it was shocking, infuriating, as an educator to hear colleagues tell Black and Brown students to get an education and get out: get out of their communities and move away from their parents and grandparents, friends, and others. The only way to be successful, these students were told, was to put distance between them and their people, to erase their connections, their history.

But, no, as Gutiérrez and Padilla clearly describe, we need the very opposite. We need our community members to lean in, weigh in, and lead in our schools and beloved communities. *Stay and Prevail* counters the pernicious narrative that we must keep our loved ones, our people, at a distance.

We are called to lead and serve in our communities. Our experiences shape our commitment, our understanding, and our inevitable successes. We won't erase ourselves from the spaces that poured into us. We will stay and by doing so, our communities will prevail."

—**Sharif El-Mekki**, founder and CEO of the Center for Black Educator Development (CBED)

STAY AND PREVAIL

NANCY GUTIÉRREZ   ROBERTO PADILLA

STAY and PREVAIL

Students of Color Don't Need to Leave Their Communities to Succeed

 ascd

Arlington, Virginia USA

2800 Shirlington Road, Suite 1001 • Arlington, VA 22206 USA
Phone: 800-933-2723 or 703-578-9600 • Fax: 703-575-5400
Website: www.ascd.org • Email: member@ascd.org
Author guidelines: www.ascd.org/write

Richard Culatta, *Chief Executive Officer;* Anthony Rebora, *Chief Content Officer;* Genny Ostertag, *Managing Director, Book Acquisitions & Editing;* Susan Hills, *Senior Acquisitions Editor;* Mary Beth Nielsen, *Director, Book Editing;* Megan Doyle, *Editor;* Thomas Lytle, *Creative Director;* Donald Ely, *Art Director;* Lisa Hill, *Graphic Designer;* Valerie Younkin, *Senior Production Designer;* Circle Graphics, *Typesetter;* Kelly Marshall, *Production Manager;* Shajuan Martin, *E-Publishing Specialist;* Christopher Logan, *Senior Production Specialist*

All web links in this book are correct as of the publication date below but may have become inactive or otherwise modified since that time. If you notice a deactivated or changed link, please email books@ascd.org with the words "Link Update" in the subject line. In your message, please specify the web link, the book title, and the page number on which the link appears.

PAPERBACK ISBN: 978-1-4166-3202-3   ASCD product #123006   n7/23
PDF E-BOOK ISBN: 978-1-4166-3203-0; see Books in Print for other formats.
Quantity discounts are available: email programteam@ascd.org or call 800-933-2723, ext. 5773, or 703-575-5773. For desk copies, go to www.ascd.org/deskcopy.

Library of Congress Cataloging-in-Publication Data

Names: Gutiérrez, Nancy B., author. | Padilla, Roberto (School superintendent), author.
Title: Stay and prevail : students of color don't need to leave their communities to succeed / Nancy Gutiérrez, Roberto Padilla.
Description: Arlington, Viriginia : ASCD, [2023] | Includes bibliographical references and index.
Identifiers: LCCN 2023003560 (print) | LCCN 2023003561 (ebook) |
  ISBN 9781416632023 (paperback) | ISBN 9781416632030 (pdf)
Subjects: LCSH: Minorities—Education—United States. | Community and school—United States. | Educational leadership—United States. | Educational equalization—United States.
Classification: LCC LC3731 .G88 2023 (print) | LCC LC3731 (ebook) |
  DDC 371.829/00973—dc23/eng/20230322
LC record available at https://lccn.loc.gov/2023003560
LC ebook record available at https://lccn.loc.gov/2023003561

31 30 29 28 27 26 25 24 23   1 2 3 4 5 6 7 8 9 10 11 12

STAY AND PREVAIL

Students of Color Don't Need to Leave Their Communities to Succeed

Foreword:
Debbie from the Bronx

W. E. B. Du Bois, an African American intellectual and the first African American to receive a doctorate at Harvard, created a concept in 1903 that pervaded much of educational thought and still ripples through our discourse today. The idea: Only 10 percent of a marginalized community could be expected to achieve at high levels or be worth the investment into their professional education. He called this special group the "talented tenth" who were "exceptional men," "the best of [the] race that they may guide the mass away from the contamination and death of the worst."

As a child, I saw the talented tenth myth personified in real life, and I thought that there was something horrendously unfair about it. I knew the people that I grew up with, that they were smart, they were capable.

The elementary school I attended grouped us heterogeneously, and the notion of the bell curve was vigorously enforced (Herrnstein & Murray, 1994). At the earliest levels, we learned that some had "it" and some didn't. The idea of a growth mindset, that one could become smarter through different forms of teaching and learning, was missing in our daily classroom interactions (Dweck, 2008). Rather, the future paths we would take were fixed and etched in our psyches at very early ages. I can still remember Diego, who struggled with every academic task; Maria, who emigrated to the country in 2nd grade and who was reprimanded frequently when she'd use a Spanish word in place of an English one; and Noel, who was ridiculed for preferring to play double Dutch rather than basketball. Diego was the kindest student in the class, Maria had a grace and artistic ability that I recognized as a 1st grader, and Noel's rendering of poems and prose held me spellbound.

Each of my classmates had gifts that went unrecognized, dreams and abilities that died a slow death grade after grade, year after year. Even as a child, I was attuned to Howard Gardner's (1983) notion of multiple intelligences as I recognized that ability, even brilliance, came in different forms. I knew that while I could excel in academic machinations, my three classmates far exceeded my ability to demonstrate kindness, artistry, and public speaking, for example. It pained me when they struggled, and I hated that some of the students laughed and that the teacher didn't stop it. The injustices I witnessed, while not registering on a conscious level, left an indelible mark on me and my sense of righteousness, purpose, and courageous action.

Regretfully, the notion of the bell curve and fixed ability groupings hadn't changed 20 years later as I taught early on. Even more unfortunately, I, too, had drunk the Kool-Aid; that is, I had come to believe that IQ was the determinant of academic success and either you were blessed with ability or you weren't. I think it is noteworthy to recognize that we each are impacted by the environment in which we are educated. The notion of the haves and have-nots is hardwired into our education system and is the default belief system that is only changed with explicit, continuous, and courageous messaging by educators and support staff.

Changing mindsets about what is possible is one of the signature elements of systemic improvement, and it occurs when leaders take rational actions (i.e., professional learning, sharing research, providing safe spaces to demonstrate risk taking and new behaviors) *and* model in ways large and small that levels of excellence can be achieved through equity. When I signed the contract with Richmond Public Schools saying that we would meet rigorous benchmarks in a very short span of time, I modeled that we had the innate capacity as a district to think and do things differently to bring about student success. I didn't realize it at the time, but this action signified a mindset that was diametrically opposed to what had always been believed—that is, that only the "talented tenth" would achieve at high levels.

Later on, as a teacher, then an administrator, I knew with certainty that it was a fiction. Exploding this myth became the center of my leadership and informed my professional goals. My academic work and research seek to discern how to lead and teach in such a way that we create legions of difference makers.

Du Bois himself came to see the flaws in his original thesis and revised his notions of leadership from the talented tenth to "the Guiding Hundredth" and predicated this new thinking on what we might now call a collective impact strategy: "We cannot have perfection. We have few saints. But we must have honest men [and women] or we die. We must have honest, far-seeing leadership or we fail" (Du Bois, 1935, p. 173).

This book seeks to help you develop this far-seeing leadership. It will deepen your belief in the fact that we can partner with communities to supplement the services needed to grow our communities no matter where we are and that we can expand the vistas for all children. Through the stories shared here, you will see that it's possible to model not just what good teaching looks like but also what a good citizen looks like, what a caring person looks like. So much of what I know about that was formed in a beautifully diverse community in the Bronx where I experienced love and care.

I grew up in the Bronxdale Houses, a housing project that was later renamed Justice Sonia Sotomayor Houses and Community Center in 2010 to honor one of its most famous residents, with whom I attended grammar school and high school. Bronxdale was a multigenerational, multiracial, and diverse community. If I close my eyes, I can see that the Tanners are right down the hall with the Ramirezes next door and next door to them, the Pacinos. The Toders, an older Jewish family, are right across from our apartment and the folks my mother trusted to hide our Christmas toys. From them, I not only learned to dance the hora, but I always got dreidels and another holiday to celebrate getting candy.

Growing up in public housing in the 1950s and early 1960s, being raised by a divorced mom with my two siblings, and seeing few positive depictions of women of color in positions of power and influence, this was my reality. However, I was blessed with a brilliant mother and an affirming suite of experiences that mitigated the barrage of negative messages. I recall how my mother and grandmother spoke up to challenge unilateral decisions. For example, in 1st grade, they wanted all of the girls to be blonde (wearing wigs made of yarn) for a skit. My grandmother said, "Hell no!" and made my wig dark brown. My mother challenged the nun who had chastised me for not attending Mass on the day of my confirmation. She called her out for her hypocrisy and told her to speak to her about the decision as it was her doing. There were so many times that I saw courageous, albeit respectful, disobedience, and it fueled my willingness to get into *good trouble,* as Congressman John Lewis called it. As everyone who knows me knows, I continue to get into trouble to this day.

Bronxdale replicated a nursery school model created in Chicago where children were cared for on-site to help the working mothers, many of whom were single because of death or divorce. This prescience provided phenomenal learning opportunities and was influential in my aspiration of becoming an educator. Many of these brilliant teachers were from the South and had come north for graduate work at schools like Columbia, NYU, and Cornell. After graduation, some wanted to stay in New York but were unable to be hired in the New York City public schools. These amazing, extremely well-educated women—Miss Forkner, Miss Mary, Miss Pryor—became teachers in the city's daycare centers. In music, they taught us to sing in different languages, and in PE, we moved to Bizet's "Toreador Song" from the opera *Carmen.*

Economically, life was a challenge for my divorced mom, but thanks to Bronxdale, we lived in a rich community in terms of its diversity and culture. She worked two jobs and relied on my brother and me for help with chores like the laundry, which we pushed in a shopping cart down the street to the laundromat. And while my upbringing taught me compassion, if I had a wish, it would be for my mom's life to have been easier. Her sacrifices allowed her to see her little Debbie from the Bronx graduate from Harvard before she died. She inspires my work with people in communities, and I see her in these moms that are trying to make a way out of no way.

While my work wasn't done in the community that raised me, I have chosen to serve the children in similar communities. Once you've experienced a community such as this, you never lose it. It becomes a calling in your life. We can honor our upbringing in the choices that we make. We can help to instill the same sense of pride and gratitude. It is amazing that many of us underestimate the power and influence of our leadership, perhaps because there are so many times when we don't have the ability to just make things happen via fiat or edict. But I have come to understand that over the long haul, the degree to which our espoused and enacted values are manifested within an organization is one of the ways that we are able to bend the vision, culture, and ultimately norms and outcomes of the system. We are watched continuously by those we lead to see how we act in times of comfort but, more important, in times of difficulty. Are we adhering to what we profess even when challenging or inconvenient? For example, some leaders profess that all children can learn, but they believe there are conditions attached. Additionally, they may accept a growth mindset for children but not for their teachers, administrators, support staff, and parents and other community members. In changing mindsets, what you do dwarfs what you say about who can and who can't be successful. Walking that talk on a daily basis was critical for my efficacy as an instructional leader.

This book names a pernicious mindset among people in marginalized communities. It believes that in our predominantly Black and Brown neighborhoods, what we offer and who we are is inferior, so if you want your child to do better, then they have to leave. There has been a real cost to Black and Brown people as they leave to succeed in the halls of prestigious schools. For some, the toll can be paid, and they can leave intact with minimal scars. But for many, there are parts of them that are broken by the experience. That is too high a cost.

Giving back to our community can take on different meanings. I never worked in the Bronx that shaped me, but I worked in communities like it intentionally and take the Bronx with me wherever I go. I believe in this way I've never left my community. The issue presented by Nancy and Roberto is that too often our young people are forced to choose between being successful by divorcing themselves from their whole and authentic selves or being unsuccessful. Our challenge as leaders is to establish learning environments and experiences that demand that students can be who they are in their community *and* be successful in their chosen world. We need them to identify their own values and connections, to learn how to code switch without shame, and to be unwilling to sacrifice their cherished beliefs for expediency.

Much of my work as the superintendent of schools was a counternarrative for the idea that you have to leave your community to be successful. We told our children, "You can stay here and receive a stellar education, and you'll also be viewed as a whole person."

The central challenge for leaders who want to create their own counternarrative campaigns is to answer the question, How do you become a prophet in your own land? How are you able to hold up a community and convey all that it has to give in a way that galvanizes its people?

Nancy and Roberto have written this book to help you answer these questions. Both of them are living counternarratives. Nancy was a teacher and principal in her East Jose, California, community, and Roberto was a superintendent back in his home of Newburgh, New York. They share their stories of how they were able to hold up a mirror in these places, name what needed to change, but also let folks know that this is where we are but not who we are or who will remain.

Because they value the communities from which they came, Nancy and Roberto embrace every aspect of what we call "community." They are keenly aware of the challenges, but they see the beauty, humanity, brilliance, opportunity, capacity, and love in the communities from which they came. The three of us share these foundational beliefs that your home community is the birthplace of your brilliance. This belief inspires their commitment to change the world with their resilience and their courageous leadership.

There are three attributes or abilities I prize above all else: wisdom, which is having knowledge and knowing why and how to use it; courage, which is acting according to an ethical moral code, especially when it is most important to the well-being of those you serve, understanding that you do so not because you're unafraid but in spite of that fear; and acting from a place of empathy and love, which is seeing the humanity and worth of those you are privileged to serve. The three attributes guide leaders to do more, believe more, inspire more, fight more, and demand more and result in a legacy worthy of the shoulders upon which we stand.

I've often told people who've worked with me: if a child or parent doesn't have a dream, give them one of yours. With their phenomenal book, Nancy and Roberto will show you how to help the young people under your watch believe that they do not have to leave to succeed.

Deborah Jewell-Sherman
Gregory R. Anrig Professor of Practice in Educational Leadership
Harvard Graduate School of Education

Deborah Jewell-Sherman is the first woman professor of practice at the Harvard Graduate School of Education (HGSE). She served as superintendent of the Richmond (VA) Public Schools from 2002 to 2008 and built a reputation as one of the most successful urban district superintendents in the country. Since returning to her alma mater in 2008, Jewell-Sherman has served as the director of the Urban Superintendents Program and currently serves as core faculty for the Doctorate of Education Leadership Program (Ed.L.D.).

Introduction:
Leading for Equitable
Change Requires Balancing
Beliefs and Actions

I am a turtle, wherever I go I carry home on my back.

—Gloria Anzaldúa, *Borderlands/La Frontera: The New Mestiza*—

Let's have a heart-to-heart.

In school communities around the nation, our youth of color living in low-income communities are told in many simple and covert ways every day that they must leave their communities in order to be successful.

Parents hear that they must move to new communities or pay more money to send their children to high-quality daycare centers or schools. A drive to a nearby suburban community makes the differences clear. Large and well-resourced buildings shimmer just across the river or railroad, and private schools tempt the "best and the brightest" from their neighborhood schools with scholarship offers and promises of better schools. Elementary-age children compete in 1st grade to be selected into gifted education programs. Sixth graders start to hear about keeping their grades up to get into the right high school across town, and all along

1

the way, young children of color are taught to work hard so they can get out of the communities that have become the source of their identities. When these same children sit in front of their television sets, they are bombarded with stories of violence, crime, and the sadness of the places they call home, perpetuating the narrative that you must *leave to succeed*.

The *leave to succeed (L2S) mindset* is a dangerous narrative and impacts a child's story of self. Children are told that their people, their neighborhoods, their families, and their schools are "bad."

"Who am I, then?" asks the child who remains and doesn't "make it out."

These messages come with deep consequences for individuals, schools, and communities. The child who is not recognized suffers wounds to the soul and psyche that are immeasurable. The child who has to leave their home experiences deep harm, too. Schools become divided places, where some children are given resources and opportunities and others are shamed for not being good enough. Those who "escape" from their communities look back and blame those who were not able to pull themselves up and out. Politicians hold back resources from those who "can't pull themselves up by their bootstraps," and communities begin to see themselves in the image that the media has created: poor, less-than, and undeserving.

A learned helplessness and despair become the sentiment of a community, and the leave to succeed mindset is reinforced. It is reinforced in a variety of ways and a variety of languages. In our experiences, we heard

- "Nene, you can do it. Leave this place and make a future for yourself!"
- "Mija, you're smart. You are an exception. Don't worry about us. Get out and achieve better than others in our barrio."
- *"Mira, tú eres original, no como los otros. Hay algo especial de ti. Vete de aquí; descubre una vida mejor."*
- "A yo bruh, no cap! Get out of here if you know what's good for ya."

This advice was genuine. Our confidants and community elders wanted us to be successful in life and felt that leaving was the only way. Their care was sincere but misguided. Whether it was implicitly or explicitly stated, those of us who were seen as having potential to do well in life were not charged with the responsibility of contributing and investing in our home community and in the collective good. But why not us? If we could make a life for ourselves elsewhere, did we not have the skills to be successful at home?

Implications for Leadership

In educational leadership interviews, one of our favorite things to do is to push candidates to describe how they perceive an urban school setting. Specifically, we ask, "What comes to mind when you think about urban schools and urban communities? What are your perceptions? What are your beliefs about education equity?" What we are really asking is *How do you perceive us? What are your beliefs about us? Even with the best of intentions, how will you treat us?*

Responses often include a range of perceptions from "Urban school settings often lack resources" to "Urban settings are rich in diversity" to very specific challenges the candidate has faced in their work in urban schools or what they believe based on the messages they have learned over time. Not surprisingly, we have even heard candidates say that students in urban settings can't perform at high levels. Often, their perspective comes from a place of deficit, creating a space for a savior to jump in and save the day.

No matter how well-intentioned, what is immediately clear is that the candidate's deficit vantage point will impact their behaviors and interactions with students, parents, and communities. Don't hire these people.

When you enter into our community with pity, embracing a *"pobrecito* complex" (roughly translated as "poor little boy"), it positions you as the savior, the superhero riding in to help us from our harmful circumstances: our friends, our families, our neighborhoods. Even if your intent is to help us, you only hurt us more. As education scholar Pedro Noguera noted (in Cepada, 2013), "I use the term 'pobrecito syndrome' to describe those who lower expectations as a form of sympathy for disadvantaged students. But our students need empathy, not pity, and they need to be challenged" (para. 10).

We often wonder, what qualifies a person to believe they are equipped to "save" other people? What level of entitlement allows a person to think someone, even an entire community of people, needs saving from *them*?

In actuality, if people from outside our communities took the time to learn about us, they would see the beauty and richness that already exist within our communities. We do not need to be saved; what we want and need is the same access afforded to children who are privileged. We want opportunities. We want to be seen as worthy and valuable. We want to be viewed as capable, deserving individuals and communities. We want the same regard, respect, and assumption of greatness given to only a select few. We want to be loved.

We want a commitment from adults who work within our communities to intentionally shift from deficit-based mindsets to asset-based ones. When the "How do I save them?" thought creeps in, we want it to be checked and reframed into an asset-based question such as "How do I leverage the gifts in this child and in the community to enhance learning and open possibilities for this child's future?" We want every adult in our community to do everything they can to *love our children up*, as if those children were their own. We want them to use their own privilege to help our youth defy the stereotypes that wrongly portray their identity and ability to excel academically, socially, and emotionally. These are not tall asks; they are human-centered ones. When our adults have an asset-based lens and hold high expectations for our youngsters, anything is possible.

This shift in mindset requires active work to unlearn the system we were all raised in and to be able to see the way racism and other inequities exist in our systems with clarity. Do we notice

- Who is in honors classes and who isn't?
- Who has access to gifted and talented programs as well as specialized schools?
- The deep and steadfast segregation of our neighborhoods?
- The racial discrepancy between the identity and experiences of teachers and leaders and the stakeholders they serve?
- Who gets disproportionality suspended?
- Who gets positions of power and authority?
- The way women are made to appear less prepared, inadequate, and less powerful?

As Tatum (2003) reminds us, racism is the smog we breathe. The question is whether we can see it.

Overwhelmingly, this mindset exists primarily in low-income, urban settings across the United States that serve our students of color. Although we authors grew up on opposite coasts, in different communities, we had similar experiences. We have both personally experienced "saviors" when we were students and also when we returned to lead in our home communities.

This perspective reflects implicit bias. We all have biases. The question is whether we are aware of how they show up in our day-to-day decision making and implementation of the work. We understand the challenges that exist in our communities, but abandoning our communities isn't the answer.

So, when and how did we realize this was a problem?

When the people closest to us saw "potential" and advised us to leave home: "You can do it. You need to get out of here if you want to achieve and make it."

Our elders meant well. They wanted us to be successful in life and felt that leaving was the only way. Whether it was implicitly or explicitly stated, many educators do this, too, like clockwork.

Our Stories Are Their Stories

Roberto's Story: Nueva York

My parents are natives of Puerto Rico, but I grew up in New York and graduated from New York schools. I always knew it was an amazing place with a rich history and talented people. I also remember it as a place that made me tough and where I consistently heard coded messages about having limited opportunities for success. Spanglish was our native tongue. The community would say, "Papito, you are different. *Tienes que salir de aquí sí quieres echar pa' lante. Me entiendes, loco?*"

The streets had swallowed up so many of us. The education system perpetuated cycles of poverty through decades of gross inequities. I learned grit at an early age. Our hard-knock life reflected exactly what was portrayed in HBO dramas and rap songs. Nothing came easy for my family. Murder, prison sentences, and evictions were constant. Survival was real. My physical facade reflected toughness, but internally I was lost.

I identify with students who face barriers to achieving their dreams. My professional mission is to root out inequities that hold our scholars back. And that is why I have led districts in New York that reflect places I was raised. From the first day I set foot in a school district, my goal was to ensure scholars had real options and they could live their best life. If they were successful, there would not be a mass exodus after graduation like there was for my generation. Instead, students would say, "I can be a leader here. I can contribute and launch a renaissance here that my community has never seen."

Nancy's Story: East San Jose

My family arrived in this country through the great state of Texas. Through migrant farm work, we landed in the fields of California. My mom tells me stories of getting $1 a day for a full day of arching her back and picking fruits and vegetables in the hot sun. We would settle in California, and I would grow up in East San Jose— an underresourced, predominantly Mexican American community—attending schools considered to be some of the worst in the state. But I didn't know those statistics as a kid; I simply loved my home community.

Although I struggled with school, I also showed potential. And when that was noticed, I was sent to take the gifted and talented test, which I failed as a 3rd grade student. When I was noticed in high school, I was told I should complete the process to qualify for the honors class or program. But I am a homegirl. I stayed put and feel very grateful for the friends and educators I met in the "regular" classes.

Too often, our youth of color are told to "get out"—that they should strive to be one of the lucky ones who leave

to succeed, as if it is a badge of honor, and as if the class,
the school, or the community itself wasn't "good enough."

So, upon graduating from college, I went back to
East San Jose and served the majority of my career as a
teacher and a principal only two blocks down the street
from where I was raised and where my mom still lives
today.

I do this work because every child in every community
deserves to feel valued and worthy, and because we are
enough—our communities, our stories, our strength. We
should never be encouraged to leave to "save ourselves"
but to see and acknowledge the beauty that exists before
our very eyes, in our own backyard, and to understand
our role in supporting and lifting the entire community
versus only ourselves.

The leave to succeed mindset is deeply personal work to us both.
With it, we intend to introduce a new phenomenon in education that
is happening, day in and day out. It intends to push education leaders
to reexamine their own beliefs and create a new way of approaching
their work.

This conversation is complex. Our intent with sharing the vulnerability of our stories and that of education leaders across the country is
to ignite necessary discussions about how deficit-based mindsets show
up in real time and generate questions about the possibilities of asset-
based, excellent schooling for all students that wouldn't require leaving
home. We seek multiple pathways, access, and options for all kids.

To be clear, this book is not meant to serve as an argument against
school choice or an argument against "going away" to college or pur-
suing a career. It is an argument for an opportunity to choose or not to
choose, to know that there are strengths and values in one's choice to
stay in one's community or to explore outside one's home community.
It is an argument for a reality that guarantees every student has access
to the best of opportunities, with their immediate home environment
being one of those options. It is a shout-out for every story that cele-
brates the strengths and heroic members of the communities we serve,

the communities our students call home. It is a call to action for leaders and educators to create a new message—one that honors the work, history, and cultures of the people who call these places home—and it is an invitation to leaders who have left to consider coming home to lead.

Call to Action

Our educators have a moral imperative to nurture aspirations. To do what is necessary to inspire success. To make sure that our youth are not forced into hard decisions to choose home or success. To never regard a child or a community as sacrificable. The issue is never about removing access from the kid who "gets out;" it is about not sacrificing the rest.

In our book, we highlight the many ways the leave to succeed mindset persists in education and how it impacts communities of color in negative, deeply harmful ways. We discuss how the mindset inherently builds a divide between individuals, results in deficit-based assumptions, and creates a scenario where resources are directed toward those who "get out." Over time, the narrative itself becomes what Sue (2015) calls a "macroaggression"—an expanded form of a microaggression that is inflicted on a group and includes verbal, behavioral, or environmental indignities, whether intentional or unintentional, that communicate hostile, derogatory, or negative slights and insults toward people of color.

When an educational leader tells a student to "get out" or that they are the exception to the rest of "these kids," it only exacerbates the problem. In truth,

- Communities should be places people are proud of, where they want to stay or return, even if they leave for a while.
- When people take pride in their community and stay and invest in it, the community as a whole gets stronger.
- Shifting mindsets is essential to ensure that it is not a badge of honor, a sign of success, to *leave* a community, but rather that an honorable option is to stay and invest in one's home.

Let's be clear: We do not think that every single person needs to stay or return to their home community, but can you please stop telling us to go away? That in order to experience our full potential, we have to leave?

It is important for us collectively to defy this notion that, for students of color living in low-income communities, leaving means succeeding. We already possess greatness and have in us the requisite talents to be successful. Your intervention is well-intentioned, but it is racist and inadequate. Investing in us means a willingness to step up on our behalf. Instead, educators and education leaders working in our community can work to intentionally help us name and identify our beauty and richness. Help us affirm our cultural and identity-based gifts, and we will excel. Stand side-by-side with us to actively fight against the leave to succeed mindset and the pool of deficit thinking in which it lives.

Join us to

- Identify where the leave to succeed mindset persists in your school systems or communities;

- Actively counter deficit-based narratives with an asset-based approach, ensuring that every student is valued and that no one is sacrificable;

- Use storytelling and counter-storytelling as a key lever to disrupt the dominant narrative;

- Build pride in the places our children and families call home;

- Examine and push on the larger systems that contribute to and perpetuate deficit-based narratives;

- Scrutinize your role in perpetuating the leave to succeed and other deficit-based mindsets; and

- Redefine success with and on behalf of the communities you serve.

This book will overlay our practical, firsthand experience of coming back home with empirical research. We will also feature the stories of many past and present leaders who have experienced this mindset in real time.

It is our hope that bringing attention to this hidden yet prevalent macroaggression will help educators who work in our communities, and the community itself, actively change this narrative. Through this examination, we also hope to engage leaders in supporting parents and students living in low-income communities so that they are able to perceive home as a place worthy of their investment and commitment.

We will also present practical leadership strategies that can be leveraged to build new cultures and systems of learning.

No one is truly served by the deficit-based narratives that have become central to our education systems. By creating another narrative, we lift up all students and communities, creating a strengths-based approach that serves every student, whether they ultimately decide to leave the places they call home or not.

We seek to defy this notion so that every student in every classroom and in every school community feels valued and affirmed and understands both the challenges and potential that exist within communities that for too long have been shamefully underestimated. Together, let's stay and prevail.

SHOULDER UP

1. What does it take to disrupt centuries of deficit-based schooling in low-income communities of color? Think about who you are and where you were raised. Did you experience more of a deficit- or asset-based mindset as part of your schooling? Articulate what that looked or sounded like to a colleague, friend, or family member. Push yourself to listen to a diverse set of stories outside your comfort zone, and compare experiences.

2. What would it mean for our public education system to provide our students the experiences of private school students and families? Engage in a school walkthrough with a private school teacher or school leader. What do you notice? What do you wonder? What do you commit to learning more about in order to level the playing field for students who attend public schools?

3. How do we redefine and embrace a new definition of success for schools, students, and communities? How do you define success? Think about the ways in which your definition either disrupts or perpetuates notions of success attainable to only a select few. What mindsets need to shift to cast a wider net and create more access and opportunity? How are you and your work personally implicated?

Leave to Succeed (L2S) as a Deficit Mindset

Get out. Vete de aquí. *Do anything you can to leave.*
Create a better life. But not here, elsewhere.
Leave and you will succeed.

For people like us who grew up in predominantly Black and Latinx low-income communities, that was the message. While we were both, per traditional measures of success, considered to be "average" students, adults saw potential.

Adults' perception of who we were was often dichotomous. When we struggled or got into trouble, we fit right in. There was nothing the adult could do because we were a lost cause. But when we showed even glimmers of potential that the adults would take credit for instilling, they would try to "save" us.

- "It's too rough out here for smart kids like you."
- "I knew you were different from them."

- "If you just keep behaving like I know you can, you can make it out of here and have a good life."

Plainly and simply put, well-meaning educators caused us and our families harm. Sometimes, it was through coded language. Other times, the message was explicit. But the takeaway was clear in either case: we were an exception to the rule and showed enough potential to be able to *leave to succeed.*

Supreme Court Justice Ruth Bader Ginsberg, culturally known as the Notorious RBG, knew this was true. She frequently paid homage to the Notorious B.I.G. as he famously rapped about stories of his upbringing. This was underscored in his first breakout single, "Juicy," where he says, "I'm blowing up like you thought I would, call the crib, same number, same hood. It's all good."

But from the perspective of an education *savior,* it was never going to be "all good" for "students with potential" to stay put. We needed to turn our backs on the same communities that raised us. The same communities that taught us. The same communities that had developed the character traits and mindsets that made us successful.

Perhaps this "if you want to be successful in life, get out" narrative persists because communities like ours are harsh for children. Examine decades of research and you will find that communities that need the most get the least. U.S. school systems in communities that serve our most vulnerable youth are the least funded, employ the most inexperienced teachers, and maintain facilities that are the most dilapidated, among a host of other factors.

In an article called "Education by the Numbers," Yin (2017) described some of the following inequities in the U.S. education system:

- Across the nation, districts with the most students of color receive 15 percent less per student in state and local funding than the whitest districts.
- Schools with high numbers of Black or Latinx students have at least twice as many first-year teachers as schools with low Black or Latinx enrollment.

The COVID-19 global pandemic elevated these and so many more inequities. A noteworthy irony is that educators in suburban school districts often used the same homes they encourage us to leave as training ground for themselves. New teachers frequently earn their stripes in "the hood" before leaving for higher pay, a shorter commute, graduate school, or an entirely new profession. As a result, those urban school districts have many more first-year teachers and higher turnover rates than their neighboring suburban districts.

Staffing inequities are not the only problems for schools with high numbers of students of color. In 2018, TNTP, an education organization committed to ending educational inequity, published the results of a study titled *The Opportunity Myth*. In this study, they revealed several striking inequities in the school experience:

- While more than half of students brought home As and Bs, students demonstrated mastery of grade-level standards on their assignments only 17 percent of the time.

- Four out of 10 classrooms with a majority of students of color never received a single grade-level assignment.

- Forty percent of college students, 66 percent of Black college students, and 53 percent of Latinx students were required to take at least one remedial course in college.

The reality is that even when students are achieving well on every assignment set before them, students of color, and particularly Black and Latinx students, have far less access to challenging, grade-level work.

In 2021, TNTP responded to the national conversation around *learning loss* catapulted by COVID-19 with a call to action for educators: *Accelerate—don't remediate.* TNTP reinforced this message with startling but not surprising data. The report found that remediation, though intended to reduce students' struggle with grade-level content, actually causes students to struggle more with grade-level material. For example, in schools with mostly students of color, nearly one in six students were remediated—regardless of their success on grade-level content earlier in the year. In addition, teachers were less likely to believe that students of color and those from low-income families were ready to engage with grade-level work.

These studies continue to confirm the impact of adults' bias-based beliefs on day-to-day practice and decision making for students, especially students of color. Factors such as ZIP code, race, gender, language proficiency, special needs, and socioeconomic status determine everything from levels of access to rigorous curriculum to how our youth experience public schooling every day. Those long-held biases and deep-seated deficit mindsets portray a child's education story long before the child arrives on the scene.

Rather than allowing these facts to stand as a picture of what *is*, they should be a catalyst for courageous change and a call to action for legislatures, policymakers, school leaders, and school system leaders. Yet leaders rarely act this courageously on behalf of young people of color. Self-proclaimed "equity warriors" engage more in trusted circles and share provocative tweets on social media but in real time can be averse to risk. Others are not aware that such inequities exist. And in the worst cases, some choose to maintain the inequities because they benefit from the status quo, either failing to recognize their own privilege or not wanting to risk losing it.

Where is the leadership? Where are the brilliant individuals most qualified to compassionately and urgently lead the changes our communities need to level the playing field and make educational equity real? We need more examples of leaders like Father Greg.

Father Greg, an American Roman Catholic priest of the Jesuit order and founder of Homeboy Industries, recognized in the early '90s, a period in Los Angeles known as the "decade of death," that it would not be wise to isolate gang members who demonstrated potential to get out of their hood and do something better in life, but rather to design business opportunities where gang members could transform their lives and positively give back to the community. What began as a way of improving the lives of former gang members in East Los Angeles has evolved into the largest gang intervention, rehab, and reentry program in the world.

Father Greg made intentional efforts to challenge the leave to succeed mindset by building capacity and cultivating leadership within the communities that mattered to those he was called to serve. He knew that what was needed was already there—that the "something" our communities needed was *us*.

The persistent problem, however, is that most leaders are not like Father Greg. Most galvanize the select few who are uniquely qualified to escape. Get out of your "hood." Leave Newburgh as fast as you can. These were our stories, too.

Sal Sí Puedes

Eastside San Jose, the predominantly Mexican American barrio where Cesar Chavez organized in the late '60s, was a neighborhood once known as "Sal Sí Puedes"—*Get out if you can.* The leave to succeed mindset literally became so ingrained and persistent that the community itself had been named to reflect the mindset.

For example, many of our colleagues who were raised in the Bronx shared that the term "Dirty Bronx" was often used as a reference to their community. It is not a label they made up for themselves, so where did they hear it and why did they repeat it? And how are schools actively perpetuating or breaking down these harmful labels? These mindsets create internal and external fears and perpetuate internalized oppression. Our federal, state, and district policies reinforce these labels by identifying schools and communities as the "most dangerous," "turnaround," and "lowest performing" and then layer these labels with a "pull yourself up by your bootstraps" mentality, ignoring the deep-seated inequities that have lived in communities for centuries, refusing to acknowledge that in the United States, it is not only about effort but also about confronting racism, xenophobia, classism, and ableism.

The fact is that our country does not value communities of color or communities living in poverty. The sad truth is that many in the education sector do not either. Even when we blast mission and vision statements saying we do. But these are the neighborhoods we call home.

Despite how deeply these mindsets were ingrained, we knew there was something wrong with this messaging. We loved our homes. Our people were there and would be there long after we would leave. These were the places we had our birthday parties, where we played spades and dominoes into the late hours of the night, where we experienced our first kisses and our high school dances. These were the places that were *familiar* to us, in the most basic sense of the word—our communities represented *familia*. These were the places we knew and loved.

So, why would we, and students everywhere, be encouraged to leave the communities we know and love?

Because the leave to succeed mindset is pervasive and baked into our educational DNA. Deficit mindsets about our homes and our communities are normalized and embraced as fact.

So What Exactly Is the Leave to Succeed (L2S) Mindset?

L2S is a deficit-based, adult belief system, most often found among educators serving students of color living in low-income communities, that

- Normalizes failure as the default outcome for the vast majority of students in these communities,
- Recognizes the achievement potential of a small subset of students living in these communities, and
- Requires permanent escape from their communities as a condition for this small subset of students to achieve success.

What does it look like?

1. The adult conveys a message that separates the individual student from the community at large, simultaneously devaluing the entire community's worth. In a conversation with a parent, the educator says, "There is something special about your child. I will help you get them into a 'good' class, program, or school."
2. When a student hears the "you are better than the rest" message, there is a risk that they may internalize and adopt the bias-based beliefs about their home community. The student may think, "I need to abandon my friends, my school, and my identity if I want to be successful."
    - The most politically correct, completely unaware form sounds like "You have tremendous potential. If you leverage this opportunity, you are capable of one day going to a place like Stanford and raising your own family in the Los Altos Hills."

- The most harmful receipt of this message feels like "You're way smarter and more capable than these ghetto people. Get out of this dump and do better for yourself and your family."

3. Students then not only carry those beliefs with them but also potentially perpetuate that belief system by sharing it with others, adding layers of credibility given their community membership. In the new class or at the new school, the student may think, "I am very lucky to be here; the students who attend the school I once attended don't have a chance. I am grateful my potential was recognized."

4. When these messages are heard multiple times from multiple adults, the entire community is at risk of internalizing those beliefs and collectively creating a space undervalued by both insiders and outsiders where the only option to achieve success is to "get out." One school and neighborhood gets labeled "bad" and the other "good." These perceptions become aligned to identity and create divisions within schools, as well as among schools. It quickly becomes apparent who has potential and who can be sacrificed.

Despite what may feel like good intentions, the L2S mindset is not one that fosters hope. It fosters a level of individualism based on fear and fueled by bias, both explicit and implicit. It reinforces negative stories of self and community.

It is the labeling of entire communities, couched in day-to-day niceties, that most concerns us—and it's done with a smile and authentic concern for the student who is "not like all the others." This labeling in turn creates a form of self-hatred and internalized oppression, taking away pride in self or in one's community, and instead fueling a desire to leave the community in order to do right by one's family and future.

The Impact of the L2S Mindset: Learning to Hate Ourselves Even More

When students hear comments reflecting the leave to succeed mindset, they can experience it as a validation of existing internalized oppression or as a microaggression they reject. But even when the receiver is aware of it as a microaggression, the repeated nature of this message can lead to deep internalization.

Carter Woodson (1933/1996) wrote *The Mis-Education of the Negro,* a seminal book widely recognized for the following position: "If you make a man feel that he is inferior, you do not have to compel him to accept an inferior status, for he will seek it himself. If you make a man think that he is justly an outcast, you do not have to order him to the back door. He will go without being told; and if there is no back door, his very nature will demand one." This quote aptly describe the power of internalized oppression. The pervasive nature of racism in the United States is so powerful that the oppressed start to believe the myth of inferiority. In the famous "doll tests," an experiment conducted by Black psychologists Kenneth and Mamie Phipps Clark that played an important role in the *Brown v. Board of Education* school desegregation decision, most of the African American children said they preferred a white doll over a Black doll. Even more troubling, some of these Black children actually ran out of the room crying when they were asked which one of these dolls looked like them (Blakemore, 2022).

Internalized oppression rarely involves a person of color screaming from a mountaintop, "I am inferior to white people!" Instead, there is a subtle yet powerful belief in centering whiteness as more normal, more desirable, simply "more." Internalized oppression looks like "skin bleaching," where darker-skinned people use creams and treatments to make their skin look more like the white default standard of beauty. Gonzalez (2019) found that although all Latinx people experience various forms of discrimination, discrimination is enhanced based on skin color. The impact of colorism included being labeled not smart; others being suspicious of them or fearing for their personal safety; being treated unfairly in the hiring, pay, or promotion process; being stopped without cause by the police; and so forth. Another example includes unwritten "brown paper bag" policies that have denied Black Americans admission into historically Black Greek letter organizations to anyone whose complexion exceeds the darkness of a brown paper bag. Internalized oppression also looks like first- or second-generation immigrants ridiculing newcomers from their country of origin as "fresh off the boat." It looks like straightening naturally curly hair and Americanizing an "ethnic-sounding" name. But to someone struggling with internalized oppression, these behaviors may feel *normal.*

When the language of the leave to succeed mindset is spoken to students of color who already unconsciously believe the myth of their inferiority and assign an unjustifiably high status to proximity to whiteness, this affirms their sense of self-hate. It feels and sounds *normal*. Running away from their communities full of people who look like them makes the same level of intuitive sense that the Black children running away from dolls exhibited in the doll study. Internally oppressed students believe they are defective because of what they see in the mirror. As a result, when educators tell them, "You're not like these other kids," this comment contributes to an inadvertent but prideful shunning of their peers and their communities.

L2S as Educational DNA: Rooting Back to Desegregation

It is impossible to separate the leave to succeed mindset from a historical and cultural context that has solidified the idea that success for the poor is to be found elsewhere. There is a reason the theme song to *The Jeffersons*, a TV show about a poor Black family who "made it," was "Movin' On Up." They "finally got a piece of the pie," so instead of being "down" in their working-class neighborhood in Queens, they were now "up" in a fancy apartment on the Upper East Side of Manhattan, living side-by-side with wealthy white people. Similarly, Outkast's third single on their debut album Southernplayalisticadillacmuzik, "git up, git out, and git something," has strong roots in the desegregation movement.

Few would refute that the desegregation movement—the forced legal racial separation of children in schools—is inherently unequal. Our communities of color encountered racism, segregation, and inequity in ways that reflected microcosms of the larger American story. When it comes to students of color, the desegregation movement relays a problematic hidden message that creates the foundation of the L2S mindset: Black and Brown students must have proximity to whiteness to experience academic success. Forced desegregation through busing, magnet schools, and other programs intended to integrate schools created an illusion of disrupting inequities and opening access. But at what cost?

Prior to desegregation, redlining and other discriminatory laws forced successful people of color to remain in their communities. Teachers at segregated schools often looked much more like the students they served. This meant that young people saw mirrors of success. It was normal for someone in their neighborhood to make it. Educational excellence was a common community expectation. W. E. B. Du Bois opined on this point as early as 1935 in his essay "Does the Negro Need Separate Schools?" Sonya Horsford (2011) detailed the consequences of forced integration in her powerful book, *Learning in a Burning House: Educational Inequality, Ideology, and (Dis)Integration*. A key takeaway from reflecting on segregated schools from the perspective of students of color attending these schools is that when there was no option to leave, there could be no notions of leaving to succeed. These communities and the schools in these communities were valuable cultural centers, spaces of affirmation and possibility.

Without question, segregated schools still faced significant challenges. Dr. Martin Luther King Jr. (1968) highlighted some of the same inequities that exist in these neighborhoods today in his "Where Do We Go from Here?" speech. He noted that Black students in elementary schools "lag one to three years behind whites" and receive far less funding. So yes, separate was inherently unequal. But it is more important to understand that *unequal* was and still is inherently unequal. During the same time period, McDonald (2017) identified places with concentrated Latinx communities that faced a persistence of subtractive language policies and curricula and tracking of Mexican American and Puerto Rican students into vocational classes. According to TNTP's 2018 *Opportunity Myth*, these ills continue to plague our education system today.

However, instead of fixing the inequities in funding formulas and equitable school resources, we have continued to pour lots of social and political capital into forced integration. We bused children out of their neighborhoods. We forced them to leave to succeed. We took the onus off of school and school system leaders to create the exceptional places of learning they would want for their own children, and instead we pat ourselves on the back for plucking a few out.

Combating L2S by Rejecting Micro- and Macroaggressions

One way to combat internalized oppression is to create the space for and intentionality around cultivating pride in identity. Students with a stronger sense of self-worth and sense of pride in their community, cultural, and racial identity hear the L2S mindset language as a microaggression versus a truth. Sue (2010) defined a microaggression as "the everyday verbal, nonverbal, and environmental slights, snubs, or insults, whether intentional or unintentional, which communicate hostile, derogatory, or negative messages to target persons based solely upon their marginalized group membership."

Most often, microaggressions go unnoticed by the person delivering them.

These actions made by multiple educators over time impact a community of people—creating a macroaggression. A macroaggression is "an expanded form of a microaggression which is inflicted upon a group and includes brief and commonplace daily verbal, behavioral, or environmental indignities, whether intentional or unintentional, that communicate hostile, derogatory, or negative racial slights and insults toward people of color" (Sue, 2010). For example, when Black and Latinx males are repeatedly treated as if they might be dangerous, they experience these everyday microaggressions as a macroaggression.

Often, educators are unaware of the immense harm or pain their words and decisions cause individuals, as well as an entire people, but these hurts add up, eventually affecting the mindsets that people hold about themselves. When adults communicate to young people that they should leave their communities in order to be successful, a self-aware child with pride in identity and community might ask, "Why?"

Combating L2S by Tackling Implicit Bias and Explicit Bias

Entering communities with a deficit-based mindset means starting from what is perceived to be lacking. An asset-based perspective, however, builds on the strengths that inherently exist in our young people. But even when we maintain an asset-based perspective, we still bring our biases with us. The key here is for educators to admit and own that every single one of us has them based on our lived experiences. The work then becomes about building awareness and recognizing how both implicit and explicit biases play out in real time.

The Kirwan Institute (TNTP, 2018) at Ohio State University describes implicit bias as "the attitudes or stereotypes that affect our understanding, actions, and decisions in an unconscious manner. These biases, which encompass both favorable and unfavorable assessments, are activated involuntarily and without an individual's awareness or intentional control." At Harvard University, an effort called Project Implicit provides individuals with tests that they can take to become more aware of their own implicit biases. A series of photos and words flash before the user's eyes, and they respond by pressing keys on the keyboard, providing insights into the user's own implicit biases. This can be a useful tool for helping people to become aware of their biases.

In education, implicit biases affect teachers' and administrators' day-to-day beliefs and actions, creating endless ramifications for students. Studies have shown that non-Black teachers have significantly lower expectations for Black students, and Black male students are four times more likely to be suspended than their white male peers for the same offenses. Black and Latinx students are less likely to be screened for gifted programs than White or Asian students, and students with disabilities are almost twice as likely to receive an out-of-school suspension than their peers without disabilities. All of these outcomes and data points are the result of educators making decisions based on their beliefs about students.

Implicit bias holds the majority of the space and discussion in the education sector, but there is a larger elephant in the room: explicit bias. Educators do not just subconsciously decide that a student who would be considered "a passionate advocate" in an upper middle-class white community is "willfully defiant" in Black and Brown classrooms. No invisible force controls educators from calling a child who asks lots of questions "inquisitive" and the other child from *that* neighborhood a "constant distraction." This is racism, plain and simple. And it is impossible to separate the leave to succeed mindset from this place of explicit bias.

If you are looking for further proof of the undeniable bias behind the L2S mindset, hold these two ideas in your head at the same time:

- White educators encourage our high-potential students of color in high-poverty communities to leave in order to be successful.
- Yet white educators move to those exact same Black and Latinx communities to find success for themselves (and while they are at it, gentrify the neighborhood).

Home ownership was and still is the number one source of wealth creation and upward mobility. Thus, the inability of people of color in these communities to participate in this economic benefit because of explicitly racist housing policies is a systemic inequity. Explicit bias explains how we end up in a place where we can tell white educators from outside these communities to move into the community to succeed while telling poor kids of color they need to *leave to succeed.*

The leave to succeed mindset cannot exist without the implicit bias that influences this belief. It would die a fast death without the explicit bias that perpetuates this viewpoint. Any time an adult tells a young person he or she must leave to succeed, bias is lurking behind the seemingly well-intended advice. To the child encouraged to leave, the bias says, "You are not like *these* people. You are better. You deserve more." And to those who stay behind, the bias says, "You are not worthy of what others are worthy of. You are less than they are."

Neither of these messages is one we want our young people to carry with them through life. Don't all students deserve the best of opportunities and chances at promising lives? Shouldn't all children be able to stay where they grew up and know that they will be guaranteed the best that we have to offer? What if the message our young people of color in these communities heard was not "git up, git out, and git something" but "get up, stay in, and *give* something"?

Why the L2S Mindset Must Become a "Kitchen Table" Education Issue

Plain and simple, the leave to succeed mindset handpicks "the chosen ones" to condition their success on leaving their homes, but the consequences of leaving home can be damning, especially as these children enter adulthood.

Not only do many students of color who leave their home carry trauma from the experience, but there is a risk that the L2S mindset continues to live deep within them as they form their own families and navigate life. For example, it could cause reluctance to send their children to a school that is "too hood," even though they turned out successful going to a similar school during their own upbringing. Or it could create adults who cannot fathom living in—much less raising children in—a neighborhood like the neighborhoods that shaped major parts of who they are. Most significantly, adults might see all of this as completely *normal.*

It is unsurprising, then, that the leave to succeed mindset is not a major theme in academic scholarship or education leadership conversations. Without question, there are amazing leaders and scholars of color leading some of the most critical education equity conversations needed today. But if these leaders and scholars are veterans of a leave to succeed experience, this, again, feels completely *normal.*

But L2S is not normal. We need to reverse this painful example of miseducation. This plea is both important and urgent. It is important because the idea of choosing a few "winners" out of a select group of students of color to succeed by having more proximity to whiteness perpetuates racism and will never be enough to create the equitable outcomes our school systems are fighting for. And it is urgent because it creates deep, harmful, and lifelong trauma for our young people who do leave.

A common leadership philosophy we believe in is that for the challenges that matter the most to any organization, community, or school system, the answers are almost always already in the room. If we are truly committed to asking and answering the hard questions needed to make education equity real, we have to realize the absurdity of telling our future community leaders to leave the room.

Homegrown Leadership Is an Option, Too

The current truths are that

- Inequities exist.
- Young people of color are frequently encouraged to leave to succeed as the *only* pathway to success, with many experiencing harm in this cycle of mixed messages and bias.

It doesn't have to be this way.

According to Andrade (2002), the point of education is not to escape poverty but to end it. However, if these same children yield to the sensitive advice to leave, how will these institutional structures be dismantled? How will or can we turn this deficit-based narrative into a strengths-based one so that our schools and communities become the heart of our work, not stories to be left behind?

Moreover, the answers to these critical questions cannot be rooted merely in hope. The leave to succeed advice given to young people is a misguided approach. The single act of leaving is a frivolous illusion and actually reinforces stories of hopelessness and pessimism. What if the answer isn't to leave? What if the answers are rooted in valuing, protecting, lifting up, and growing our home communities? Or, simply, what if there are multiple pathways to success that can include staying deeply connected to your identity and home community?

It starts with how we educators envision and describe the places our students call home.

Coming Home: Sí, Se Puede

Lisa Delpit (2006) suggests that many academic problems attributed to children of color are actually the result of miscommunication, as primarily white teachers and "other people's children" struggle with the imbalance of power and the dynamics plaguing our system. But it doesn't have to be this way. When educators are able to see the spaces where they teach as "home" to both their students and themselves, it changes the experience for young people. They then treat their education communities as places they value and can see the beauty of, and it changes the way in which they interact with their students.

It starts with the stories we tell and the messages we send. It starts when we, both white educators and educators of color, are able to see the world around our schools as home to the students we serve and when we are able to take an asset-based approach to the communities we serve. As Dolores Huerta, civil rights icon and activist who rarely receives credit for coining the famous slogan *Sí, se puede* (Spanish for "Yes, we can"), teaches us, "People can take power over their communities and over their lives. Some people don't realize that they can do that. They think it is OK for other people, but I myself can't do it."

Can we imagine a world where we lift up stories that are different from our own? Where we leverage an asset-based approach to engage with students and communities? Where we tell our youth that returning home to serve the very community that raised you is a noble and excellent example of success? It sounds easy, but to do this, we must actively confront our own biases and create systems and structures that build the adult capacity to engage and interact differently than the status quo.

If we are willing to do such, we would be willing to see past the facade of concern and create deeper connections with groups of people who are different from us. We would ask students, "If not you, then who?" We would create a continuum of pathways students could take, one of which would be to do as Mahatma Gandhi suggested and "be the change" they wish to see in their own communities. We wouldn't impose our own beliefs and values onto students but allow our students and communities to define success for themselves.

Education, no matter where in the nation it is provided, should improve life outcomes for all students. However, the realities tell a different story. ZIP codes and parents' education levels continue to be predictors of the destinies children will face. How could this happen?

Leaving to succeed is a flawed myth. It is built on a set of beliefs that get reinforced daily with our youth, ones that hold no merit or truth but are loaded with well-intentioned racism and classism, perpetuated in our school systems each day. Instead of *sal sí puedes,* we want to reinforce *sí, se puede!*

This should be every child's right—to grow and learn in the place they call home and to know that anything is possible because of this opportunity. Leaving is not bad per se, as long as staying to give back isn't framed as bad, either. Our young people deserve options that do not perpetuate neglect and unhealthy cycles of poverty and miseducation in their home communities.

We have a long way to go. To ensure our students have these opportunities, we as education leaders have to take a stand. We can start by collectively challenging the leave to succeed mindset—in our stories, in our leadership, and in our own personal acts of courage.

SHOULDER UP

1. Where does the L2S mindset show up in the community you are called to serve? Notice it in teacher and leader talk. Do you hear it in staff meetings? Do you see it in images on the walls that don't reflect your student community? Take a walk around your school and see where the L2S mindset shows up.

2. What messages are you implicitly or explicitly sending your students about their families and communities? It's easier to do than you might think. For example, as principals, we heard teachers advocate for specific students to get out of their class because they deserved better (blaming the other students). The teacher meant to be helpful but at no point took responsibility for the type of environment they were cultivating within their classroom or the level of education they were providing to every single student. Instead, they wanted to pluck one out and stay the course, inadvertently perpetuating the L2S mindset. Have you or a colleague ever had such an experience, where you thought you were helping but maybe upon reflection realized that you were perpetuating the L2S mindset?

3. How are you caring for and building the capacity of the young people of the community you serve, as if they were your own? This is rhetoric commonly stated by well-intentioned adults, but what does it really mean? What do you want for your own child or children you love? Literally, create a list. How is that vision you just listed connected to or disconnected from the education you offer at your school or in your school system?

Leading Cultural Change on Parallel Paths: School and System

Define success on your own terms,
achieve it by your own rules,
and build a life you're proud to live.

—Anne Sweeney—

Enacting cultural change, for schools and systems alike, will require redefining traditional measures of success on a large scale but, more specifically, for students of color living in low-income communities. This is critical because enacting change requires challenging the status quo as well as practices that perpetuate painful and deep-seated deficit mindsets, including L2S. A literal change in direction is needed at this time, and it must be done on two parallel, simultaneous paths: school and system.

L2S as a One-Way Street

For drivers, a One Way street sign indicates a traffic pattern to be followed. For some youth, the same sign might represent the leave to succeed message, as in success is available just one way—and that way is out of their neighborhood.

But what if instead of One Way signs telling us we are either in or out, we have access to multidirectional streets? If the adults in our lives, especially in our schools, had actively fought against the L2S mindset, then we authors would have been raised knowing that we deserve the option to leave to pursue whatever we wish to pursue while also knowing that returning is another equally viable option. The imagery provided by a two-way street is like a bird's nest. Fledglings see the mother bird leave the nest regularly, but she always comes back. She may need to leave the nest to get things that the nest does not have, but she always knows the way back to the nest.

Moving back and forth, coming and going, leaving and returning are all notions that normalize reciprocity in relation to one's starting point, base, or home. But in the L2S mindset, our youth are encouraged to go one way and never to return. So they leave. Get out. Escape. Run to the end zone and score.

To challenge this approach, we ask leaders to embrace an explicit way of leading that combats L2S and deficit-based mindsets like it, by applying the four-part NEST framework (see Figure 2.1):

1. **Name the ugly:** Unapologetically name and recognize the existing dysfunctional paradigms and harmful messaging that infiltrates communities of color in the community you are serving. You cannot change what you cannot name. Say it publicly.
2. **Explicitly flip the ugly:** Unlearn existing archetypes and cultural ecosystems in order to challenge behaviors and mindsets about the definition of success, and then reframe the conversation.
3. **Shoulder up:** Leverage leadership as a key to igniting and encouraging a renewed set of adult behaviors that honor our communities. Therefore, stand tall, lift your head with pride, and collaborate with the community by, figuratively and literally, standing shoulder-to-shoulder.

Figure 2.1 NEST Framework

Part	Significance
1. <u>N</u>aming the ugly	Unapologetically naming and recognizing the existing dysfunctional paradigm and harmful messaging that have infiltrated communities of color.
2. <u>E</u>xplicitly flipping	Unlearning existing archetypes in order to challenge existing behaviors and mindsets about the definition of success, recognizing brilliance in underestimated communities, and sharing counternarratives of success frequently and widely.
3. <u>S</u>houldering up	Igniting and encouraging a renewed set of adult behaviors that honor our communities; naming reinvestment in one's community as one of the greatest future investments a community member could make—and providing various pathways to success, beyond traditional measures.
4. <u>T</u>ransitioning the power	Embracing this work as for the community and by the community, not trying to be a superhero.

4. **Transition the power:** Remember that this work is meant to be for the community, by the community, not you. Even if you are from this community, the power belongs to the people. Transition the power.

This chapter will unpack each of these phases in an education leader's quest to interrupt deficit-based mindsets such as L2S and enact cultural change, whether at the school or system level.

Phase 1: Name the Ugly: Unapologetically Name and Identify Deficit Mindsets

Because context matters, messages about L2S will look and sound unique in different communities. To start, leaders must identify the problem before they change it using a proactive, bold approach to identification.

Plainly put, if we don't see it and name it, we cannot address it. We also cannot change what we are willing to tolerate.

This does not suggest that leaders engage in a typical, run-of-the-mill leadership listening-and-learning tour where they visit and learn about the community in order to create a guide for their 90-day entry plan. We are encouraging something much more progressive.

Instead, create the space needed to *name the ugly*. The goal here is to get a pulse of the community by deeply understanding all the ways that this community has been harmed. How do we identify the internalized oppression imposed on low-income communities of color? What learned language does the community use to suffocate its hopes and aspirations? For example:

- What explicit racism, classism, or xenophobia has the community experienced? *Be willing to go into the heart of the community to hear the pain.*

- What are all the messages and stories that have been told to the community, in one way or another, that they are not good enough? *This will get uncomfortable, but the community needs to speak their truth. Listen intently and reflect back what you're hearing.*

- What are the key deficit-based themes that have been deeply perpetuated over time and now regularly live in the community? *Know that underperformance has never been about ability but about low expectations as well as a narrow definition of success. Be a strategic ethnographer.*

Here are two powerful vignettes demonstrating the "ugly" you are looking for:

Vignette 2.1: Backhanded Compliments
Former Superintendent Susana Cordova

Nearly 30 years after she began her career in her hometown of Denver as a bilingual teacher, Susana Cordova was selected as superintendent of the 92,000-student school district in December 2018.

Being from the community, she knew personally what biases and beliefs existed about the parts of the community that represented her experience.

As a student growing up in this community, I would always receive backhanded compliments such as "You're not like the other kids" or "You're so successful and different from others in this community." I was told by so many that education was a ticket out of my community as if my community was not good enough.

There is nothing inherently bad about our communities. Our low-income communities of color have a strong emphasis on family, connection, and support. I wouldn't be in this role today if I didn't have strong family and community support—throughout life, they would drop what they were doing in a heartbeat to help and support me. And I would do the same for them. They, literally, would give me the last shirt off their backs. There is nothing like home.

We don't hear these asset-based messages enough. Instead, we hear more demonstrations of "the ugly."

Vignette 2.2: "Here, Our Girls Get Pregnant"
Former Principal Nancy Gutiérrez

As a principal in my barrio, only two blocks from my childhood home, I had the privilege and honor to work with several veteran teachers who had dedicated their lives to serving East San Jose, one of whom was Mr. Headapohl, a war veteran turned 8th grade algebra teacher who was originally from Michigan but had taught in East San Jose for decades. Mr. Headapohl was a compassionate teacher and a staple of the community—someone whom students returned to campus to visit and someone who would continue to do whatever he could to support and lift the community, in the ways he knew how.

That said, every time Mr. Headapohl would have the opportunity to speak about our majority Mexican American community in public settings, he would start with "This neighborhood, 95122, has the highest teenage pregnancy rate. Here, our girls get pregnant." That was his consistent line and message—and it typically had nothing to do with what we were talking about at that moment. It certainly had nothing to do with algebra.

Latinas still have the highest adolescent birthrate in Santa Clara County, though rates have declined as a whole, and East San Jose adolescents remain especially vulnerable.

Although Mr. Headapohl's facts were not wrong, why did this single story guide his thinking and mindset about the community? What did adolescent pregnancy have to do with algebra, and why did he leverage every chance he got to "announce" it and normalize it as part of our community's story?

Does internalized oppression play a role when we start believing and acting upon the distorted messages about our in-group? What if instead of these messages that sometimes become self-fulfilling prophecies, students heard a different message? What if Mr. Headapohl said that girls in the community rise to the challenge? That they understand how to operate under tremendous constraints? Or that they are responsible, resourceful, and resilient? This is not meant to downplay the challenges of raising a child as a school-aged teenager. But Mr. Headapohl's language, "Here, our girls get pregnant," was an explicit One Way sign: leave to succeed.

There are so many similar "backhanded" messages, as Cordova called them, delivered on a daily basis. What we, as educators, haven't gotten good at yet is actually talking about them without using coded language. If we are to surface and identify what is really happening, we cannot use coded language. Period.

Effective leaders create the space for communities to speak their truth, which means speaking to their anger and pain. It means sitting in discomfort and creating spaces for healing and reconciliation. This physical space may vary. It could be at the community center, in a school, in a church, in the mayor's office, at the district office, or in someone's living room. The only prerequisite is that we as leaders need to be willing to truly listen and internalize what is being shared. Go to the people, in the intimate spaces they value.

As Singleton (2015) helps us decipher in *Courageous Conversations About Race*, identifying where we are on "the compass" helps us understand one another's opinions and beliefs.

- Emotional: What are you feeling?
- Intellectual: What are you thinking?
- Moral: What do you believe?
- Social: What will you do?

As a school principal, Nancy would frequently say, "When we speak of our youth and our families, we will consciously and intentionally use asset-based language." In the case of Mr. Headapohl's misguided and consistent messaging, a leader might have called it out explicitly: "Mr. Headapohl, why do you continuously talk about adolescent pregnancies as our community's single story? Our community has many talents, skills, and positive contributions. Do you realize the impact your deficit-based mindset has on our youth? At this school, we will tell the story of our community through an asset-based lens. We will no longer give a one-sided depiction of who we are."

Speaking one's truth is only useful when creating such a space to identify the active harmful messages swimming about in the community. The truth is that in our formal leadership roles, we are often afraid to engage in *real talk* because if we truly listen to the pain that exists, we will have to do something about it.

Tatum (2003) talks about racism and inequities being in the air we breathe. In *Why Are All the Black Kids Sitting Together in the Cafeteria?* the first chapter is appropriately called "Can We Talk?" Tatum compares racism to smog: "Sometimes it is so thick it is visible, other times, it is less apparent but always day in and day out, we are breathing it" (p. 6). Even if leaders wanted to put their heads in the sand to escape from their responsibility to name the ugly, eventually they will suffocate themselves as deficit mindsets seep into all parts of life.

Here are some key questions to unpack experiences and pain that cut through the smog:

- Tell me about the horrible [racist, classist, xenophobic, differently abled] stereotypes that people believe about your community. Which are most painful? Why?
- Tell me about the painful experiences you or your family personally experienced with teachers, schools, principals, or the district office. What happened? How did it make you feel? How did it permanently impact you and your family?
- When have you felt unseen, unheard, and undervalued?
- What do you love about your community that the rest of the world doesn't see?

We are tempted here to add a question about the ideal state: "If you had a crystal ball, what would an ideal relationship with the school or district look like?" But doing so would be premature and presumptuous. We move to solutions too quickly sometimes, to the detriment of actually hearing and lifting the voices of our communities.

To start chipping away at deficit-based mindsets, we actually have to see and name them explicitly. Leaders must be willing to sit with the pain of the community and create authentic spaces for sharing and healing. As a school leader, you represent every school leader with whom a person has interacted. Even if you have great intentions in your role, the pain will be projected onto you. Own that. It is only your fault if you choose to hear-to-respond instead of listen-to-understand. You do not have to have all the answers; you just have to be willing to hear the pain in their words. Picture yourself in their shoes. The same is true for our system leaders.

Phase 2: Explicitly Flip: Intentionally Recommunicate and Reposition

The next step gets even harder.

To truly enact cultural change, leaders must take all the pain of the community, very plainly, and flip it on its head. That's right: leaders must convert miseducation, commit to reeducation, and create opportunities for unlearning and experimenting with new ways of interacting and being. Leaders cannot do this without trust.

Knowing that the initial conversation cannot be the only conversation, especially after asking a group of community members to spill their guts, you must have the courage to go back for a second round. It is not a cameo appearance. In this setting, you want to make sure stakeholders feel heard without trying to make excuses for the adults in the school system, getting defensive, or glossing over the pain. It is thus important to repeat back to the community, very explicitly, what you heard. It is equally important to, as Harvard Kennedy School professor Marshall Ganz (2012) says, balance urgency with hope.

As you share what you heard them say, it is important also to explicitly share your beliefs. Specifically, name that you don't believe the deficit-based messages that reinforce ideas about "these kids can't this" or "these kids can't that." Know that our low-income communities of color have been flooded with negative messages about who we are and what we are capable of for centuries. It is deeply and traumatically ingrained. And although you may not have created the inequities and harm that exist within the communities, you are responsible for addressing and attending to them. They are deeper than any one moment or any one leader. So say, straight-up, "I don't believe these assumptions made about us." Yes, as the leader, you are now part of the "us." Leaders enact cultural change when they create an "us" with the community they serve and when they model what it means to explicitly flip deficit-based language and beliefs (see the examples in Figure 2.2). "Us" represents *familia*. It represents a team approach.

The idea of explicitly flipping language seems like a technical solution to an adaptive problem, but it isn't. This requires real work and real

Figure 2.2 Flipping the L2S Mindset

What I heard you say	L2S mindset translation	Explicit flip
This place is "sketchy"and "dangerous."	Follow the One Way sign out because, although you are one of the good ones, this place is not where children like you should end up.	I hear you expressing fear of what you don't know. Visit us and get to know our beautiful community.
Their parents don't care.	Follow the One Way sign out because kids like you will never get enough support from your families.	A parent who sacrifices and risks everything for their child is the definition of caring.
These kids are the bottom 5 percent. They struggle to learn basic concepts.	Follow the One Way sign out because kids like you will never make it if you are in an environment with struggling students. Instead, attend school in a different community with successful students.	Your definition of success is too narrow. What are the variety of ways we can celebrate the success of our students? If kids struggle to learn, then we need to change how we teach and question whether learning is relevant, responsive, and engaging.
College isn't for everyone.	Follow the One Way sign out because kids like you have a chance to be something. These other kids don't.	Our colleges would be lucky if our students chose to bring their talent, resilience, and experiences to their campuses.

courage. You may be surprised at how triggered some get when we simply flip language to be fairer and more equitable or representative of a collective aspiration that levels the playing field. There are politics even in language, but the goal here is to explicitly flip long-held messages to create sources of empowerment.

Consider these examples of flipping or reclaiming language:

- The Black Lives Matter movement, founded in 2013, advocates for nonviolent civil disobedience in protest against incidents of police brutality. It highlights the problems uniquely facing our Black community in the same way we highlighted amyotrophic lateral sclerosis (ALS), also known as Lou Gehrig's disease, with the ice bucket challenge in 2014. The goal was to elevate the issue versus saying other issues didn't also matter. Yet, contrarians proclaimed that "All Lives Matter" because it became too uncomfortable to *name the ugly*. The analogy would be to disregard the attention garnered for ALS and instead advocate that "all diseases matter."

- Mexican Americans have used the word *Chicano* to describe people of Mexican origin living in the United States since the early twentieth century. The term was originally used as a pejorative, a way to describe Mexican Americans of lower social standing, but in the 1960s, the term was flipped and became a point of pride connoting a deep understanding of a Mexican American's political standing in the United States. Still, the pushback against the actual term, even within the Mexican American community, is far and wide, with some noting that it creates division and others noting that it is a separation from one's Mexican roots.

- The term *queer* came to be used pejoratively against LGBTQIA communities, but beginning in the late 1980s, queer activists began to reclaim the word as a deliberately provocative alternative and source of pride.

Consider, as well, the journey of language to describe a person of color. It has shifted in a variety of forms—from "colored" to "minorities" to "people of color" to "BIPOC"—and continues to evolve as an effort to empower, heal, and reconcile language. As Oluo (2018) reminds us in *So You Want to Talk About Race*:

> Looking at American History, words have been used to separate, dehumanize, and oppress, and the power of those words is still felt today. Picture a water fountain with the word "colored" on it. Picture a lunch counter sign depicting, "Whites Only." Picture a group of angry white men encircling a terrified black boy screaming "white power." Think of the words used to subtly signify race. Words like ghetto, nappy, uppity, articulate, and thug. All these words can conjure up powerful emotions because they remind us of the powerful history and present that they have helped create. People of color have inherited the pain of these words.

In education, the politics of language, similarly, comes with an immense amount of pushback. Take the example of former chancellor Richard Carranza of the New York City Department of Education (NYCDOE) in his journey to shift from deficit-based "English learners" to asset-based "multilingual learners."

Vignette 2.3: Multilingual Learners Versus English Language Learners
Former Chancellor Richard Carranza

As part of Chancellor Richard Carranza's Advance Equity Now initiative in 2019, he took a keen eye to students who were learning English as a second language. When he entered the NYCDOE, students were referred to as "ELLs," an abbreviation for "English language learners."

Carranza, who is Mexican American, leveraged his story of self to speak about overcoming challenges as an English language learner himself in his early school years. He emphasized that speaking a native language other than English is an asset, not a deficit. "English isn't my first language, and when I was younger, I did question whether I could compete with all these students whose first language is English. The answer very quickly became, 'Absolutely I can compete.'"

The new term he would introduce to the largest school system in the country: *multilingual learners*. Carranza repositioned the work of supporting multilingual learners to create the space for students to learn a new language and achieve their greatest potential without sacrificing their home languages and cultures. "I stopped referring to folks as English language learners. I call them future bilingual learners or future bilingual students or multilingual learners." In his first year as chancellor, Carranza would announce the addition of almost 50 bilingual education programs.

This "flipping" initiative didn't happen without a tremendous amount of pushback, but in the end, not only does the entire NYCDOE system refer to once-called "ELLs" as "multilingual learners," but the country caught on as well. This new asset-based language is setting a trend for the world to see.

Another example of explicitly flipping language is when schools or school systems shift from calling youth "students" to "scholars." This positive label positions our youth as successful, naming their assets and potential from the start, which is typically what happens in wealthier communities.

Vignette 2.4: Students as Super Scholars

Former Principal Roberto Padilla

Roberto was a first-year principal in Manhattan. He was appointed midyear to support a young middle school on the verge of shutdown. Families were fleeing the school, and the media had named the school "lawless."

Despite some of its earliest struggles, the most troubling observance was how adults depicted children who attended the school. At the time, the New York City Department of Education decided, by way of policy, that newly created schools would not be permitted to screen children. This sounds like a solid policy—except that this middle school was the only school in the entire district that could not screen. Consequently, parents, families, and even students started to refer to the school as a "dumping ground."

When Roberto heard this term, he would consistently push back and ask, "What do you put at a dumping ground?" The answer was always "Trash." Roberto would then ask, "Why would you refer to children, someone's child, as trash?" He was "naming the ugly" in ways others didn't want to hear.

Roberto knew that real cultural transformation was not going to be a mandate from his seat. Instead, he explicitly flipped it by giving the school community a new language. He said, "From here on, we will refer to all students on this campus as 'scholars' and not 'those kids.'" In addition, he named students achieving grades of 85 percent or higher in their classes "super scholars." He explicitly flipped and defined the new language and modeled behavior reflective of high expectations. By doing this, he challenged his school community to value the scholars for the genius and the greatness that had always existed in them.

Explicitly flipping is about leveraging an asset- and relationship-based approach above all else. If leaders actively nurtured and affirmed students and families through an asset- and relationship-based approach, then we could collectively instill a YCMAD ("You can make a difference") mindset as well as a deep level of confidence to support students as they navigate the world with a stronger balance of treasure and trauma.

Phase 3: Shoulder Up: Leading Un-Learning with Courage

As leaders engage in this courageous truth-telling process, the big question becomes "Now what?" How do you use this information and these conversations to inform your leadership at the school or system level? And how do you stay connected to the ground-level challenges that earned you the trust and respect you deserve after engaging in real talk and real listening with the community?

For far too long, disenfranchised communities have struggled with false prophets who bribe and seduce our communities with education reform ideologies. It's time for advisors who are community driven, not ego driven.

So, what's the antidote to deficit-based practices and specifically L2S? How do we get people to value the richness, even if struggle is involved, of their home communities? What are we going to do about it? How do we unlearn, galvanize voices, and change the existing culture with humility? How do we shoulder up?

Lebron James spoke about his home community of Akron, Ohio, in his 2020 graduation speech during the COVID-19 pandemic.

> In places like Akron, Ohio, schools are an essential service. . . . Our schools are our safety net, our people build our communities. . . . Your community needs you. And when I say your community, I mean your church, your youth group, but most of all, your school. They need you. Most importantly, building your community is how you change the world. Unfortunately, the system does not solve the real problems: education, violence,

racism. These problems must be solved in the streets. I know the last thing you want to hear is to "stay home." My message is to "stay close to home." Maybe not physically but in every way possible. . . . Be the first generation to embrace a new responsibility to rebuild your community. You will determine how we rebuild. Make your community your priority. (Vera & Hayes, 2020).

Vignette 2.5: "I Promise" Initiative
NBA Player Lebron James

In 2017, NBA star Lebron James defied the L2S mindset by investing in his community. Alarmed by the high school dropout rate, he worked with the Akron School Board to launch the "I Promise" initiative.

James struggled as a student in Akron. His mother didn't have a permanent job, which forced his family to move multiple times and led to him being absent from school for 83 days in 4th grade (Seale, 2018).

We all know he became famous through an extraordinary basketball career, but instead of celebrating his "escape," he used his success to help others in his hometown.

> I know these kids basically more than they know themselves. I've walked the same streets, I've rode the same bikes on the streets they ride on, I went through the same emotions, the good, the bad, the adversity. Everything they're going through as kids I know, and for me to be in a position where I have the resources, the finances, the people, the structure, and the city around me, why not? (Seale, 2018)

James considers the founding of I Promise School (IPS) as the most important professional accomplishment of his life. The LeBron James Family Foundation supports children and families attending IPS with uniforms, food for families, career placement services, bikes and helmets, transportation, and GED and job placement services for parents.

In addition, free tuition to the University of Akron for every graduating student is covered under scholarship. To qualify for IPS, students must be one to two years below grade level. IPS challenges students with a rigorous STEM, hands-on, problem-based learning focus. According to author Colin Seale (2020), James is

> making tremendous strides toward closing the critical thinking gap. . . . LeBron's school recognizes what any asset-focused educator already knows: so-called "at-risk" students typically have more critical thinking capacity than their more affluent counterparts because they so regularly have to think on their toes, assess credibility, and innovate around constraints. But they too often lack access to classroom spaces designed to unleash their inherent critical thinking potential. The I Promise School is challenging this troubling narrative by closing the critical thinking gap on day one.

As part of a true partnership, the Akron School District will bear more than half of the costs—presumably around 75 percent—once IPS is fully running to serve grades 1–8.

Not only did James *shoulder up,* but he also ensured the work was part of the community and owned by the community—that is, he *transitioned the power*—the last step of the NEST Framework. We don't want "saviors;" we want partnerships.

Shouldering up includes owning the responsibility to teach activism, community organizing, and leadership as part of this work. It means letting go of the monopoly about who owns the power over this community. It means sharing. It means accounting for the treasure that exists in communities, not just the trauma.

As Veronica Crespin-Palmer, Lead Executive Officer of RISE Colorado, says, it is not only about adding a seat to the table but potentially getting rid of the table altogether and "circling up" for an authentic discussion. Superintendent Susan Cordova embodies this philosophy, cultivating leadership in the youth of Denver Public Schools every year with Challenge 5280.

Vignette 2.6: Challenge 5280
Former Superintendent Susana Cordova

5280 represents Denver's elevation. It is also the name of a student voice and leadership program where every school has a team that works on a yearlong problem of practice that culminates in a policy recommendation to Superintendent Susana Cordova and the school board.

One year, for example, a youth group worked to improve water quality and was able to install filtered water across the school. Another year, a student group worked on improving relationships with police officers, after identifying the first interaction with police officers as a problem. These students realized it was typically negative and created an immediate barrier between the two groups. Students therefore organized a march from their school to the local police station and partnered on a barbecue and dance-off to build relationships and help make the first interaction positive.

Challenge 5280 allows Denver youth to take on and own problems that they are experiencing in their own communities. It is a student-led and student-driven endeavor that first takes a look at their immediate school environment and then considers wider implications and solutions in order to have greater impact.

2019's winner identified the mismatch between students and teachers in terms of race, culture, and identity. In response, students put together a yearlong professional development program for teachers on Zaretta Hammond's (2015) *Culturally Responsive Teaching and the Brain*—and teachers participated!

This work has continued despite Cordova's departure and, every year, is action oriented and tangible. Most important, it "gives the work back" to stakeholders and creates the agency to change things directly that don't work in their world, not directed by the district but with its support.

Vignette 2.7: "We will not hold low-income students back a grade because of coronavirus"
CEO Sonja Santelises

Sonja Santelises worked for 25 years for urban school systems as an administrator and educator. Since May 2016, she has served as the CEO of Baltimore City Public Schools (BCPS).

In 2020, the COVID-19 pandemic hit. Communities of color across the United States were disproportionately affected. In 2020, BCPS itself was 76.6 percent African American, 13.5 percent Latinx, 7.6 percent white, 1 percent Asian, 0.2 percent American Indian, and 0.2 percent Pacific Islander.

School districts across the globe scrambled to find the right approach to support their students and families socially and emotionally while not losing sight of their core task as educators: teaching and learning. It was during this time that Santelises penned an op-ed titled, "We Will Not Hold Low-Income Students Back a Grade Because of Coronavirus." She explained, "In Baltimore, where I lead the city school district, life has been turned upside down for the vast majority of the families we serve—many of whom were inadequately served to begin with. More people are food and housing insecure, many more are unemployed. Mothers stand in long lines simply to secure a package of diapers" (Santelises, 2020, para. 2).

Like other school systems, BCPS moved quickly to create new supports for students and families, including distance learning grounded in high-quality curricula. In this effort, Santelises named one big topic of interest and conversation: retaining students to account for unfinished learning given the interruption of schooling due to the pandemic. Her response was to call it a "desperate measure" and explicitly name that this measure would predominantly impact low-income students of color.

Further, Santelises unpacked what it means to retain students during a typical year that does more harm than good to our youth.

Consider how retention might play out in practice: for instance, the implications of using a single blunt assessment to decide who should be left back; the imperfect logic of focusing on low-income students, some of whom are performing above grade level; the role that bias might play in deciding who is left back; the role that parent advocacy might play in deciding who is advanced. The likely practical outcome of this extraordinarily expensive approach—$15,000 per student at Maryland's current spending rate—will be to burden large groups of students already adversely affected by segregation with lowered expectations and even more segregation. (para. 6)

Disagreeing with the harmful practice of retention, Santelises argued that it was important to double down on two things that have always worked well for our youth: (1) strengthening relationships and (2) ensuring access to a strong curriculum. Her rationale is an example of not only naming the ugly but explicitly flipping it so that stakeholders understand the antidote needed to combat a punitive and dysfunctional culture

Santelises ended her op-ed with a call to action: "To the armchair policy elites who essentially want to give me $15,000 for every student I damage by holding large groups of them in the same grade another year, I say this: give me those funds to accelerate our instructional work and focus our collective creativity on testing and rapidly scaling new evidence-based solutions" (para. 11).

Just naming the ugly doesn't do the job if not explicitly flipped with the alternative. At the same time, without naming the ugly, stakeholders won't understand the "why" behind the decision to do something countercultural. Leadership requires standing shoulder to shoulder with the community, and it takes courage to do so knowing that it will create a great deal of discomfort.

When you "shoulder up" with the community to enact cultural change, you will notice how everyone picks their heads up, pulls their shoulders back with pride, and stands shoulder to shoulder with you to get the tough work done.

Phase 4: Transition the Power

Creating a two-way street that challenges the one-way L2S mindset is a requirement for asset-based leadership. Positional power, however, is not a requirement for creating this two-way street. In fact, if leaders fail to adequately yield the floor to community members, this hoarding of leadership may further affirm the ugly messages that lead to the L2S mindset. To be clear, transitioning the power is not about empowering the communities you serve. These communities have always had power. They had power before you arrived or returned there, and they will have power if and when you leave. This is about boldly galvanizing and mobilizing their power as a leadership priority.

Janice Jackson, former CEO of Chicago Public Schools (CPS) from 2017 to 2021, exemplified this boldness with her launch of an alumni office and program to leverage the leadership of thousands of alumni who graduated from Chicago Public Schools. "Greatness has been cultivated in CPS. Getting some of our successful alumni to share their stories in an effort to motivate our scholars to see the greatness that was cultivated here firsthand. We want to reach the everyday person and make success attainable as well as create easy pathways to support local schools through fundraising, days of service, and the like" (Masterson, 2021). When Jackson moved on from CPS, she founded HOPE Chicago, a scholarship organization that promises to "redefine the education landscape" in Chicago. Funds will go toward providing scholarships for approximately 24,000 first-year college students over the next decade, as well as giving aid to 6,000 parents or guardians who are also seeking to continue their education (Masterson, 2021).

Whether through returning to lead your home school district or managing a scholarship fund, there are so many ways to give back and reinvest in your home community. Indeed, if education leaders create space for reinvestment in their communities through activism, community organizing, and leadership, then students will have multiple pathways to "give back" and leverage these tools to lead at home or in representative communities.

In this theory of change, leadership shows up in a variety of ways, and cultural change takes place because we have changed the parameters and the rules. Success then does not *only* mean physically returning to one's neighborhood to serve as a teacher, principal, or superintendent. It simply means creating two-way streets: give and get. Here are a few ideas:

1. **Grab the Mic:** Tell everyone what makes your community special. Highlight the strengths of your community to as many people as possible. What should others know about your home? Treat it as a treasure hunt. Pass the mic to the unelected mayors and unappointed leaders of your community to have them share your community's magic as well.

2. **Benjamin Franklins:** Invest financially—contribute to a community effort from your own pocket. Start a scholarship fund for hometown youth. Work for a philanthropic organization that invests in your home community or similar communities. Spotlight existing formal and informal ways communities take care of each other financially, including when you pass around a special collection at church or fundraise teenagers who need uniforms for their sports teams. Every single person who contributes is a powerful investor.

3. **Volunteer:** Mentor or coach youth who are from your community or similar communities. Or mentor the adults. As a leader, be humble enough to also seek out mentorship from a community steward.

4. **Do the J-O-B. Teach! Lead! Organize!** Go back home and become a teacher or a leader. Create the type of school practice and systems you wish you or your family and friends had had. Run for office or school board. Advocate for a change in policies affecting your community or similar communities. Do not be a leader who says, "We just need the community to. . . ." You are part of the community. Be the change.

Vignette 2.8: Renaissance Academy of Arts, Science, and Social Justice
Founder and Former Principal Nancy Gutiérrez

After parent Maria Gonzalez walked into my classroom to observe me teach a 7th grade social studies course, we would sit down for a debrief.

> *Gracias por venir. Como hice? Que hice buena y que debo hacer diferente?* Thank you for coming. How did I do? What would've made it better?

Expecting to have a conversation about my class and how her son Pedro was doing in it, I was thrown off that she didn't want to have either of those discussions. Instead, she wanted to talk to me about my beliefs and values aligned to education in our community. About her own ideas. And about a house meeting that would take place that night a few blocks down the street.

Maria was there to organize me.

Maria was part of a faith-based collective that had been meeting with local community organizers, People Acting in Community Together (PACT), and had identified inadequate schools as among the group's deepest concerns.

As part of this effort, PACT had arranged for Spanish-speaking parents across East San Jose to visit small schools in New York City and Oakland. When they returned, they set out on a few concrete next steps to create the school of their dreams—the schools they wished their kids would've had the opportunity to attend, the schools that the wealthy had access to—"Why couldn't we have the same in East San Jose?"

Of course, Nancy attended the meeting that night.

That experience was one Nancy will never forget. The house was packed, and parents were speaking their truths. She took copious notes, and Maria followed up, this time bringing additional parents to ask Nancy to lead an effort to create a new small middle school. In the next few weeks, East San Jose parents chose her to lead the design and development of a school of choice—working not with a superintendent or a district administrator, not even PACT, the community organization shepherding this effort, but families. And the most touching thing was that even parents like Maria, whose own children would be too old to attend this dream school, would work like mad to make it happen. This was for the *comunidad*.

With tremendous advocacy and support from the community as well as community-based pressure placed on school board members and the district superintendent, the group eventually opened three new small schools of choice in 2004: LUCHA, Renaissance, and Adelante. Renaissance Academy of Arts, Science, and Social Justice was founded in 2004 in the Alum Rock Union School District by the community and for the community:

- 280 students; 6th–8th grades
- 81 percent Latinx; 10 percent Asian
- 80 percent low-income

After only two years, Renaissance would become a California Distinguished School and a Gold Ribbon School a few years later. Renaissance remains among the top 10 percent of Silicon Valley middle schools for low-income students in both English and math.

Though coming home to serve is not the only pathway, it represents the highest level of return on investment and the truest badge of honor. It is important that young people be given the opportunity to defy the leave to succeed mindset and see their home as a place where their talents can be invested and why our country and (especially) our distressed schools would be stronger for it.

What does it look like? It looks like

- Creating space for students to understand the rich history of their communities as well as their own family's story and journey into the community.
- An explicit effort to support student in the intersections of their identity.
- A collective narrative of strength and activism.
- Igniting dreams and hopes as contributors of society without letting go of their identity or language.
- Culturally affirming spaces where asset-based messages are shared and heard multiple times by multiple adults.
- A community that knows and understands the power of its worth and value—and a deep care for the beautiful communities that raised them.

Leading Cultural Change
Means Redefining Success

Success is liking yourself,
liking what you do, and liking how you do it.

—Maya Angelou—

What if, instead of leaving to succeed, we encourage our youth to look within the room, within the community, and in their very backyards for the answers? Take Hilda Maldonado, superintendent of Santa Barbara Schools, for example.

Vignette 2.9: All You Have to Do Is Look in Your Backyard
Superintendent Hilda Maldonado

Hilda Maldonado, superintendent of Santa Barbara Unified School District (SBUSD) and former associate superintendent of the Los Angeles Unified School District (LAUSD), was never told to leave to succeed. Born in Mexico, she immigrated with her family at the age of 12. She was raised in Montecito Heights in LA's Highland Park. The community was known for The Avenues (Los Avenidas), a street gang whose roots traced back to the 1940s, originally as an initiative to support Mexican American youth from violence. Unfortunately, Los Avenidas turned the corner in the 1960s during the heroin and cocaine epidemic, beginning to engage in criminal activities and becoming the notorious gang they are known as today.

Still, the community itself, despite its problems, instilled great pride in its people. Not only did Hilda attend Franklin High School, a very racially and economically diverse school, but she had a teacher named Rocky Delgadillo who had left East Los Angeles to attend Harvard University only to return as a teacher in his home community. Delgadillo was the barrio's golden boy and an example of what it meant to go outside the community to grow yourself and then return home to give back.

The overall theme in Hilda's community endorsed reinvestment in and pride for their community. For example, the local Catholic church would encourage college graduates to attend church with their cap and gown and speak to the congregation to share their success. The congregation would acknowledge and celebrate them when they returned. So, when Hilda graduated from Cal State–Los Angeles, she came to church in her cap and gown, stood in front of the congregation, and said, "Yes, this is about going out to experience the world, but I think it is important to serve the area where you come from." Hearing this, the community cheered her on.

Inspired by Mother Teresa, Hilda recalled the sister's response when she was asked about going to Calcutta to help in India: "All you have to do is look in your backyard." Hilda would dedicate her gifts and talents to the Los Angeles community, working in every role throughout the school system as she rose the ranks to become the associate superintendent of LAUSD, the second largest school system in the United States.

Los Angeles is home to a lot of pride—so much so that several educators within LAUSD are from the 720 square miles that encompass the community at large. "We have so many diverse leaders who have experienced different communities," Hilda says. "It's not unlikely for those who work here to be from here." It also helps that Los Angeles is home to so much rich cultural history. Before Mexican Americans became the political and cultural force that they are now in East Los Angeles (where they have also been the dominant ethnicity for about 60 years), the neighborhood went through a series of anti-Mexican sentiments—from the Zoot Suit riots of the 1940s, to Cesar Chavez moving the headquarters for the Latino civil rights group the Community Service Organization to East Los Angeles in 1958, to the 1960s when East Los Angeles became an epicenter for political and social activity during the civil rights era and especially for the Chicano movement.

> As the largest Mexican population outside of Mexico City, East Los Angeles is full of cultural pride—a representation of a community's strength.

We often share so much about the deficit and the trauma that live in our communities, but there is equally as much diversity and resolve in our community. Through this pain and trauma, we have strength. We are resilient people. These are communities whose citizens have pride in saying where they are from.

We cannot promise that defying the L2S mindset will be easy and painless. We are certain, however, that if you engage in this work as we have described, then schools and school systems will be better and do better for the communities they serve. When schools do well, communities prosper.

It is our hope that, over time, it will become less about how the system defines success but how the scholars and families define it. How do we shift the culture to where our scholars truly see their treasures and worth, where it is not up to the system to determine how "good" or worthy they are or how much potential they have—but it is about the community rising up with great strength and pride in who they are and what is possible?

SHOULDER UP

1. As a leader, how will you leverage the *NEST Framework* to lead cultural change at the school or system level? As a first step, identify an accountability partner and share your plan with them. This gives you additional eyes and ears on your plan before revealing it publicly to a wider audience. Know your blind spots.

2. How will you explicitly *name the ugly* and bring to light the harmful messaging that infiltrates the community you serve? In a conversation with families, students, and/or community members, ask questions to get to the root of their experiences. Then, repeat back to them what you literally heard.

3. How will you *explicitly flip* the inequities you surface by leveraging counternarratives? When you hear deficit-based thinking, address it in real time by flipping the message on its head. And then, ask for feedback about how it landed.

4. How will you *shoulder up* and stand with communities to ignite and encourage a renewed set of adult behaviors that honor the assets of the community you serve? Work with stakeholders to collectively define success. What does it look and sound like? Break down any definitions that are too narrowly defined (for example, test scores only).

5. How will you *transition the power*? Create a project that names the various ways community members and graduates can give back to their community, making it an easy and accessible option for all. Reflect and revise your process frequently through community-centered feedback.

Defying L2S in the Instructional Core: The Brilliant School

Education is everywhere and the political goal
of education for people of oppressed groups,
must be aimed at finding a means
to end their oppression.

—W. E. B. Du Bois—

What is an asset-based classroom, and what is it not? Where does the leave to succeed mindset show up in the instructional core? The term *instructional core* has been defined as "teacher and student in the presence of content" (City et al., 2009). The *relationship* among these three elements, and not the qualities of any one element, determines the nature of instructional practice (Figure 3.1).

Figure 3.1 The Instructional Core

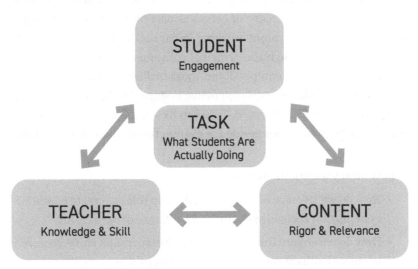

Source: Adapted from City et al. (2009).

We extend the concept of the instructional core to consider the entire school environment and its impact on instructional practice. In our construct, everyone in the school system is implicated. Indeed, transforming a student's educational trajectory does not fall on one person's shoulders but on the entire system of educators in the school building, thus defined as *school* and *student* in the presence of *content*.

A Wallace Foundation–commissioned report by Grissom and colleagues (2021) followed up on the 2004 findings from the foundational Leithwood Report, which categorized leadership as second to teaching among school-related factors that improve student achievement (Leithwood et al., 2004). Nearly 20 years later, the researchers found that the principal is in fact as important as the teacher in their impact on students, but with greater scale and reach.

We have been classroom teachers and principals and can personally attest to how leadership roles shape the lives of young people. "It is difficult to envision an investment in K–12 education with a higher ceiling on its potential return than improving school leadership." In addition, several prominent education organizations extended its reach beyond the school principal and implicated the entire system. The Leadership Academy (TLA), formerly the NYC Leadership Academy founded in 2003, revamped its theory of action as part of its five-year strategic plan to extend to the system, working in parallel with the school. TLA understood that although the principal continues to be a key lever for change, even the best-equipped and most brilliant principals will hit walls without an aligned and supportive system. As Chenoweth (2021) argues in *Districts That Succeed*, "You can fix schools all you want; if the districts within which they reside are dysfunctional, the schools will not stay fixed."

Several key questions emerge:

- How do we leverage our unique leadership roles to create education systems that recognize the unique brilliance of each child?
- How do we ensure that the necessary instructional shifts required to create brilliant schools include mindset shifts as well?
- How do we equip leaders with the ability to draw a throughline from their day-to-day decisions directly to the classroom?
- What type of classroom or schoolwide learning experiences do we want for our own children? And is that what we are giving to the school we lead?
- How do we ensure that students and families have access to brilliant schools and systems so that they do not feel like they must leave to succeed?

Personalizing these questions grounds how we teach and lead. It is not a coincidence that what we want for our own family is guided by a set of very high standards that differentiates inputs based on the needs of each child. Undoubtedly, we want the best there is for those we love as well.

To move past deficit-based mindsets in the classroom, we cannot think of the students in our schools and in our classrooms as other people's children. As Delpit (2006) teaches us, "We do not really see through our eyes or hear through our ears, but through our beliefs."

As lifelong educators, here is what we want for all children:

- We want children to be authentically engaged in meaningful tasks that are of interest and relevant to them.

- We want children to see positive examples of themselves in the curricula. For us, this would mean seeing and learning about Puerto Rican and Mexican American history and the wealth of talent within their ethnic, cultural, and racial identities.
- We want children to learn about others, outside their ethnic, cultural, and racial identities because it builds our collective capacity to exist and engage in a globally diverse world.
- We want children to have real-world experiences that can be applied immediately.
- We want children to experience the realities of society, whether good or bad, acknowledged and brought into the classroom for critical discourse.
- We want children to be nurtured, socially and emotionally, and to feel brave bringing every intersection of their identity into the classroom.
- We want children to be inspired to be their very best selves—to dream big and determine success on their own terms.
- We want children to be valued by society, inspired by future possibilities, and happy.

None of what we named is radical or impossible. At the same time, we also have to be very clear about what we do *not* want for our children:

- We don't want a classroom where our children are taught to agree with everything they read or discuss. Rather, we want them to get into "good trouble," as the late John Lewis taught us, by questioning the world in order to become innovators and critical thinkers.
- We don't want a classroom where the textbook is the primary driver of learning because learning, in preparation for life, is not that technical or clear-cut.
- We don't want a classroom where our children are forced to "sit and get" or where "good" behavior means you SLANT on demand (Sit up, Lean forward, Ask and answer questions, Nod your head, and Track the speaker; Lemov, 2010).
- We don't want a classroom to mirror what it feels like to be incarcerated, such as walking in single file-lines in the hallway, holding

their breath, or blowing air bubbles to prevent them from talking to one another as they transition to classes.

- We don't want a classroom where our children must adhere to dominant, middle-class culture in the way they think, speak, or behave in order to experience success.

- We don't want a classroom that teaches our children to devalue who they are, where they come from, and the unique assets they individually bring into the space.

We want them to be seen, heard, motivated, and challenged. We want our children to feel loved at school and be recognized for their brilliance every single day. We do not want them to feel like the only way to experience success is to leave the community that raised them.

Brilliant Classrooms Across the School System

Recognition as a brilliant student for far too long has relied too heavily on singular measures of success such as standardized testing. This often determines the level of a student's and family's access to classroom placement and opportunities such as magnet or specialized schools. But if you are not one who was chosen to leave to succeed, what are you left with?

According to Joshi Hansen (2017), in her "The Future of Smart" TED Talk, "Children walk away from their K–12 education with a good sense of the things they are not good at. This becomes part of their identity as adults." As philosopher René Descartes proclaimed, "I think; therefore I am." Joshi Hansen stated that brilliant kids debate, argue, resolve conflict, and develop empathy and compassion, and they persist because they are interested and because they care. When students have good academic struggles in the classroom, she argued, they often don't struggle with those same skills in the real world, noting that 40 percent of scientists at NASA are dyslexic and represent the "future of smart."

Yet, the leave to succeed mindset would define brilliance based on the students who get out—it doesn't matter why or how they got out, but because they did, they get categorized as "smart." In actuality, brilliant students stay, too; they are the students who are self-aware and leverage how they learn best to contribute in meaningful ways to school and life.

For example, Roberto's brilliance as a young person showed up as adaptability—he adapted in his ability to thrive in multiple environments and connect with people from all backgrounds and beliefs. Irrespective of his resources and access, he was able to connect with people in urban, suburban, and rural environments. It also showed up as athletic prowess, reflected in being identified as the captain of multiple sports teams, winning several team and individual championships. Furthermore, his brilliance showed up as perseverance, learning how to manage childhood trauma at a very young age, remaining optimistic about the future he could create.

Nancy's brilliance as a young person showed up as constantly asking critical questions of the world, such as questioning policies she perceived as unjust in school or in the community. It also showed up as activism when she spoke up against the wrongs inflicted on her schoolmates and community and had the courage to question authority on behalf of the greater good. Yet the perception of Nancy's brilliance was to label her a defiant troublemaker.

Given this frame, a brilliant teacher understands how to identify the unique brilliance of each student and is able to see through the standard, rigid, and narrowly defined perception of excellence. A brilliant principal creates a space for the brilliant teacher to thrive, creating a culture of celebrating and valuing the unique gifts each student and family bring. As important, brilliant systems create the conditions to acknowledge the unique gifts and brilliance across the community.

What New Conditions Are Required?

We can counter this message by demanding a counternarrative of truisms. For example, we can intentionally declare that

- All girls can do math and excel in science.
- Black boys who wear hoodies can be doctors.
- Multilingual learners are linguistically gifted and shape a global society.

Words matter. Beliefs matter. Behaviors matter. To understand where these words and beliefs come from, we must examine, question, and transform the mindsets that inform these words and beliefs, because whether intentionally or unintentionally, they live in the classroom and affect the daily interaction among the elements of the school core: school, student, and content.

In every classroom, school, and school system across the United States that serves majority students of color and/or students living in low-income communities, this counternarrative must be written explicitly into their theories of change.

Deficit-based mindsets must be actively acknowledged, broken down, and intentionally replaced with an asset-based perspective so that leaving to succeed is not the only option. If a thought virus can embody deficits, then we can also identify immunities like asset-based mindsets. Make strength finding a highly contagious process.

We argue along with Lisa Delpit (2006) and Chris Emdin (2016) that deficit-based schooling is manifested in a belief that students of color in low-income communities are deficient. Here's our belief: *If we leverage leadership to create brilliant schools that are innovative, asset based, community rich, and accountable to a vision for deeper learning, schools become places where kids are held to the highest academic standards while being able to bring the intersections of their identities into the school setting— including their interests, passions, and talents.*

Brilliant schools are:

- **Innovative.** Academic achievement and advancement are fueled by high expectations and a recognition that each student brings unique gifts to the school setting. Classrooms become interest driven, and the schools build teachers' capacity to become the coach, facilitator, and guide for learning. These schools focus on creative solutions to solving their communities' most persistent challenges.

- **Asset based.** When schools begin to look at what students understand, know, and can do, it changes the way teachers approach learning. In asset-based schools, families are seen as the experts of their children—individuals who know their children the best and are valued and welcomed as critical allies, resources, and partners in the education process.

- **Community rich.** Curriculum and pedagogical practice honor the fullness of communities and make students' lived experiences part of the learning process. Community-rich schools honor the ethnic, historical, cultural, and racial identity of each student through every interaction in and out of the classroom setting and create conditions for students and families to build multiracial coalitions for change.

- **Accountable to a vision for deeper learning.** Every adult throughout the system is implicated in creating brilliant schools and classrooms and therefore accepts the responsibility to set high expectations for themselves, their colleagues, and students. Students are engaged in rigorous, interest-driven tasks because the adults believe students can perform at high levels. Adults also identify multiple points of entry for each student to experience success.

Learning from City, Elmore, Fiaman, and Teitel's concept of the instructional core, creating brilliant spaces for young people requires the presence and interaction of all four of the strategies presented here. They cannot be executed in a piecemeal fashion but rather together with consistency into the daily operation of schools, to support the interaction among school, student, and content every day.

Brilliant Schools Are Innovative

TNTP's (2018) researchers found that most students—and especially students of color, those from low-income families, those with mild to moderate special needs, and multilingual learners—spent most of their school days missing out on four crucial resources: grade-appropriate assignments, strong instruction, deep engagement, and teachers with high expectations. They found that

- Students have big, clear plans.

- Most students do what they're asked in school but are still not ready to succeed, often because what they are being asked to do is not aligned to their grade level.

- Greater access to the four resources can and does improve student achievement, particularly for students who start the school year behind.

TNTP (2018) also found that when students who started one year behind grade level had access to stronger instruction, they closed gaps with their peers by six months.

So, what shifts do educational leaders need to do to ensure that innovation lives in their brilliant school? We posit that it is the educational leader's role to build the capacity of their staff to

- **Rethink learning tools, space, and time.** Given what we have learned from the pandemic, what will we decide to keep and what will we decide to abandon? The "way things have always been" no longer works for the students and families you serve.

- **Ensure a strong instructional core with multiple extensions to learning.** This includes project-based learning, connections to the arts and sciences, and deeper learning that is not offered as an after-school or Saturday program but as part of the day-to-day instructional core.

- **Normalize inquiry.** Create spaces for students and adults to question, give feedback, and leverage real-time problem solving about the issues they deem deeply important.

- **Center students as designers and executors.** Build the capacity for students to evaluate themselves and one another and for adults to act as facilitators of their learning (versus givers of knowledge).

- **Design multiple entry points for students at varying achievement levels without lowering expectations.** Allow the freedom for students to find their unique gifts, passions, and interests through the schooling process while still ensuring access to a standards-based, grade-level curriculum with rigorous tasks.

- **Encourage students to defend their thinking and arguments and to consider those of others.** Many of us were taught to get the right answer—that was the goal. However, our proposed instructional core model requires students to explain and show their thinking. The cognitive and learning science behind students' thinking reveals the what, when, and why, not just the how. When students have opportunities to analyze one another's reasoning, they are likely to improve their own conceptual and procedural knowledge.

Example 1: Genius Hour

Cultivate a school or school system where students and adults alike can explore their "genius"—their interests and passion that ultimately drive innovation for the entire system.

Genius Hour is based on Google's philosophy called "20 percent time," where employees are permitted to work on projects that interest them 20 percent of their work time. Notable wins to come out of the 20 percent policy include Gmail, Google Talk, and Google News. In adapting this to the education setting, superintendents like Dr. Rhoda Mhiripiri-Reed of Hopkins (Minnesota) Public Schools ask students, teachers, and leaders, "What if you could learn about anything you wanted?" Genius Hour requires school leaders to prioritize a movement of inquiry-based and learner-directed activities as Superintendent Mhiripiri-Reed has done as part of the district culture.

Example 2: The Harkness Table

Cultivate a school or school system where students and adults engage in rich and critical discourse as a means of problem solving, where ideas are explored and learners develop the courage to speak, the compassion to listen, and the empathy to understand.

Phillips Exeter Academy's Harkness method, established in 1930, is based on the belief that learning should be a democratic affair where a small group of students and one teacher sit around an oval table and discuss content. This strategy is used in every content area, requiring minimal teacher intervention and a lot of student ownership in guiding the discussion forward. This concept is aligned to the Coalition of Essential Schools' Common Principle #5, which names student-as-worker and teacher-as-coach. Students learn how to work independently and solve complex problems over a period of time with guidance from the teacher to identify the initial problem of practice—ensuring it is standards aligned and creates access to grade-level content.

Example 3: After-Action Reviews

Cultivate a school or school system where processes are consistently assessed and evaluated and a culture of feedback is built and sustained.

In the U.S. Army, after-action reviews (AARs) help provide soldiers and units feedback on mission and task performances in training and in combat. In schools, students and adults work in teams and learn how to give one another direct feedback about their performance. District and school leaders model a level of consistent and frequent reflection to evaluate all they do. Taking place at the completion of projects, an AAR asks four questions:

- What did we expect to happen?
- What actually occurred?
- What went well and why?
- What can we improve upon and how?

Example 4: Access to the Arts— Orchestra for All

Cultivate a school or school system where the arts are centered as part of the learning process.

When former principal Cris Vaughan founded Baychester Academy in the Bronx in 2010, she knew the arts were an essential piece of a brilliant school. So, she teamed up with Education Through Music (ETM) to ensure that every single student in her preK–5 school would be offered an introduction to music: learning to read music, gaining proficiency in the instrument of their choice, and the option of becoming part of the schoolwide orchestra. Through this partnership, music would be integrated into the school culture, and ETM would offer professional learning to nonmusic teachers, working side-by-side with Principal Vaughan to create long-term sustainability of the music program.

Example 5: Rethinking Schools

Cultivate a school or school system where adults and students have the freedom to dream big about how to transform schools to best prepare students for the future.

In 2015, the XQ Super School Challenge, an organization dedicated to rethinking the high school experience, invited school communities across the nation to dream big about new approaches to high school. Prior to that, the same freedom to innovate was given to leaders across New York City during the Small Schools Movement where leaders had the ability to break large schools into smaller, autonomous schools— a method that was intended to personalize learning and increase democratic participation (Meier, 2013)—was replicated across the country, including in the San Francisco Bay Area. This reform worked as one piece of a complex puzzle but certainly not a one-size-fits-all strategy.

Brilliant Schools Are Asset Based

The impact adults have on young, impressionable children can either build confidence or completely destroy it. There are not enough healthy and uplifting beliefs about communities of color and poor communities. Defying the leave to succeed mindset is our attempt to cut off the cycle of pessimistic beliefs that exist about our homes. A new set of beliefs is required. No longer can we accept that some children are broken— systems are broken, not children. The pervasiveness of low expectations ensures underperformance and self-fulfilled prophecies. Deficit-based thinking needs to be replaced with asset-based strategies.

Low expectations cannot prevail when educators understand and leverage aspirational, navigational, and social capital as assets. For example, a teacher cannot look students in the eye and decide not to give them challenging work if they know they have tremendous hopes and dreams for their futures. It is hard to argue that a student is "too low" to handle rigorous instruction once you recognize the rigor of your assignments is light work compared to the rigors of navigating the struggle. Assigning the L2S label to star students based on the neighborhood they live in would not happen if educators understood the value of social capital in that same neighborhood.

What shifts, then, does an educational leader need to make to ensure that an asset-based mindset lives in every adult's belief system in the cultivation and maintenance of their brilliant school? We posit that it is the educational leader's role to build the capacity of their staff to

- **Build meaningful relationships with every student and family.** This requires leaders to go beyond food, fun, and fiesta and engage families in ways that regard them as true partners in the work.

- **Tap prior knowledge.** Ensure content and text open the door to students' lived experiences and prior knowledge.

- **Provide opportunities for students to give feedback on the learning process.** Create structures for students to weigh in on assignments and assessments and engage in double-loop learning processes with one another and with adults.

- **Use multiple data points to assess students' abilities and needs.** Interrupt the overreliance on standardized tests by leveraging multiple forms of data such as observation of discussion, home visits, and written work, as well as formative and summative assessments.

- **Communicate assets.** Publicly describe students' assets directly to them, their families, and their communities consistently.

Example 1: Connect Students to the Assets in Their Community

Cultivate a school or school system where adults and students unapologetically foster positive self-identity and celebrate the rich legacy of their ancestors' contributions.

Fostering Black children's "positive identity development" in the way Hebrew and Chinese schools do for children in other communities is exactly what founder and former DC Public Schools chancellor Kaya Henderson had in mind when she launched Reconstruction. Reconstruction's goal is to counter a narrative that Black families don't value education by modeling how to reconnect kids to the assets of the Black community and the resiliency of its descendants. It also calls on students to contribute to the rich legacy of the Black community through authentically rich curricula.

Example 2: Elevate and Honor the Assets at Every Level of Student Identity

Cultivate a school or school system where adults and students engage in traditions that honor their identities and give back to their communities.

Eagle Academy founder and New York City Schools Chancellor David Banks created Eagle Academy for Young Men as a brave space for Black and Latinx young men to elevate the intersections of their identity using critical traditions. Examples include

- Engaging in a morning town hall where students have the opportunity to honor a person or persons, past or present, in their lives or not, through the pouring of libations. The pouring of libations involves adding water to the tree of life that young men maintain through the powerful ritual.
- Reciting the "Invictus" poem by William Ernest Henley at the end of the daily town hall to exemplify how young men take charge of their lives and their destinies.
- Being divided into houses that honor exemplary Black and Latinx men such as Malcolm X, Che Guevara, Barack Obama, and Roberto Clemente.
- Giving thanks on the day before Thanksgiving every year by hosting a celebration with a collective potluck of more than 600 staff, scholars, alumni, and families providing dishes and engaging in service.

There are many rituals that Eagle Academy leverages to honor boys and young men of color.

Example 3: Exhibiting Excellence (E2) Referral

Cultivate a school or school system where brilliant performance and behavior is honored (as opposed to perceived "bad" behavior).

As a principal, Nancy flipped the script on disciplinary practices across the school. Typically, students would get sent to the school principal for misbehaving, but instead, all students who were "exhibiting excellence" were sent to the principal for a handshake, a conversation, and a positive phone call home. Examples included everything from academics to going out of their way to help another student. Students would come into the office with huge smiles on their faces, eager to share their success stories with the principal and with their families.

Example 4: Accessible Communication for All

Cultivate a school or school system where every single person who is part of the community feels that their native language is honored and respected.

Nella Garcia-Urban of Houston, Texas, is the chief external officer of YES Prep Public Schools, which battles societal inequities by ensuring that parents in their community are seen as partners by receiving timely and empowering communication. Information to parents is consistently sent out in multiple languages, and even after the materials are translated, Nella goes back over them to make sure the meaning is clear. This intentional focus on communication allows YES parents to be more engaged and feel respected as partners. When parents are seen as assets, children thrive.

Example 5: Multilingualism as an Asset in the San Francisco Bay Area

Cultivate a school or school system where adults and students honor native language acquisition and create a culture of celebrating and promoting bilingual and bicultural school communities.

Frances Teso returned to her hometown of East Side San Jose to found a dual-language immersion school in California's South Bay Area that would give rise to Voices Dual Language Charter Schools. Today, this network represents some of the most sought-after schools in California. In 2021, every single school in this charter management network had a waiting list, and families are asking Voices to build additional schools across the state.

Brilliant Schools Are Community Rich

As proud Latinx leaders, we pay close attention to authors who can shed light on the experiences of Latinx young people. Through her stories and careful research in her classic *Subtractive Schooling*, Valenzuela (1999) named the ways schools strip young people of their identities. "*Subtractive schooling* encompasses subtractively assimilationist policies and practices that are designed to divest Mexican students of their culture and language." The students described in her book "oppose a schooling process that disrespects them," a process that creates social, cultural, and linguistic divisions, resulting in weak teacher–student relationships and a feeling of mistrust that stifles learning. Though decades old, the findings in this book are still relevant today and point to the need to embrace identity and community as part of the learning process.

What shifts does an educational leader need to make to ensure a community-rich school? We posit that it is the educational leader's role to build the capacity of their staff to

- **Build relationships with diverse community experts to inform school and classroom content.** Ensure schools do not continue to act like a fortress to outsiders. The community is the quintessential partner for improvement, and they should not have to cross a "moat" to gain access. Relationships with the community matter— so does access.

- **Teach about the harm in our history's truth and in doing so, also lift the beauty.** For example, teach about the way slavery lingers today but also about the kings and queens of Africa (Robinson, 2020). Teach about the abuse of farmworkers but also the strength of the movement and leadership of leaders such as Dolores Huerta.

- **Create space for students and families to bring lived experiences into the learning environment beyond food, fun, and fiesta.** Walk the neighborhood to understand the fabric of the community. The more authentic the school experience, the more students feel valued. This is more than just inviting students to use their prior knowledge. Educators have to be intentional about connecting the learning to the most relevant experiences students have.

- **Let parents lead.** Support parent leaders to design essential questions and a vision that empowers them to create change in their community through the schooling process. Engage in authentic conversations, truly listen, and be willing to cede power.
- **Highlight community leadership at all levels.** Engage in processes that require direct interaction with the community as opposed to tokenization.

Example 1: Be Explicitly Anti-Racist

Cultivate a school or school system centered on awareness, action, and advocacy.

Bobby White, a native of Memphis, came back to his hometown to launch the Frayser Community Schools (FCS) charter school network to support neighborhood schools. He leveraged Memphis's rich history of community activism (for example, it is where Dr. Martin Luther King Jr. fought to upend systemic racism and was assassinated in 1968) to launch an anti-racist initiative in 2020 with three critical areas of focus: (1) eliminate the school-to-prison pipeline, (2) build trauma-informed schools, and (3) increase parent engagement and advocacy.

Example 2: Connecting Content to Lived Experiences

Cultivate a school or school system where students get consistent practice with engaging in culturally responsive curriculum and instruction.

Gholdy Muhammad's (2020) *Equity Framework for Culturally and Historically Responsive Literacy* identifies identity, intellect, skill development, criticality, and joy as key levers to advancing culturally responsive practice. For example, in a 5th grade literacy module, when students are asked, "How does this connect to your life?" they typically struggle—not because they don't know how it connects to their lives but because they have an unpracticed skill of being able to make meaningful connections with school content. New York City District 11 superintendent Cris Vaughan, who partners closely with Muhammad, creates the conditions necessary to ensure students are getting continued and consistent practice. Using Muhammad's model, the district extends learning in intentional ways. For example, when studying Jackie Robinson, questions are raised not only about the moment in history but also about the intersections of his identity (Black man, athlete, civil rights leader, corporate executive, etc.). This helps students think about the power dynamics that Robinson encountered and that they too may encounter. The trick here is to leverage practice and explicit modeling as key levers for skill building on connecting content to lived experiences.

Example 3: Leveraging Community Voice to Take Action

Cultivate a school or school system where adult, student, and community voices are lifted as part of the decision-making process.

As a response to the country's reckoning with racial justice in 2020 following George Floyd's murder, former Des Moines superintendent Thomas Ahart created an opportunity for the community to speak and for district leaders to listen. The district held nine town halls over multiple weeks and then acted based on what they heard. They communicated their action steps and follow-up moves back to the community. They announced two new positions grown out of input from staff, students, families, and the community. One role was to lead a comprehensive system to support and nurture staff of color, in service of helping with retention and eventual recruitment efforts. The other role was to give employees who were ready to become new principals the opportunity to serve in the position with enhanced support from the district.

Example 4: Student Leadership

Cultivate a school or school system where leadership is shared with students as part of the school culture and curriculum.

Student leadership is part of the fabric of Ocala STEAM Academy in San Jose, California. Principal Tracy Leathers and her team have two selection processes to elevate student leadership: one set of leaders selected by the students to represent student interests and another set of leaders selected by staff to serve as ambassadors. All student leaders are expected to lead by example and serve as role models to other students as well as the community. When visitors come, students lead tours display-ing complete ownership of the school community and are able to articu-late everything from learning expectations to restorative practices in the same way one would traditionally expect of a school principal.

Example 5: Holistic Approach

Cultivate a school or school system where a holistic approach to students and families drives.

Harlem Children Zone (HCZ) is a community school that provides wrap-around services in Central Harlem—from life-shaping early child-hood, college, and career support and education programs, to life-affirming community outreach and wellness initiatives. Since HCZ's founding, its model has served more than 22,500 children and families annually within a 97-block zone. The neighborhood-wide network of programs and services includes

- Building up our youngest,
- Building up promising futures,
- Building up purpose,
- Building up professional lives, and
- Building up neighborhoods.

Brilliant Schools Are Accountable to a Vision for Deeper Learning

It was tempting to name the fourth arm of a brilliant school simply "accountability." But as our teacher and mentor, the late Richard Elmore, would always say, "You cannot hold high expectations without matching those expectations with the same level of support." Brilliant schools not only have a vision for deeper learning but also hold others account-able to it.

We consider this quality to be a critical paradigm shift. Unequivocally, schools need to be accountable to an audacious vision for improvement that centers on intellectual engagement and equitable support. Conse-quently, schools must consider their own capacity for this kind of change in leadership. A new approach for accountability in schools and classrooms is needed; otherwise, failure to adapt will result in more "accountability patchwork."

Let's go deeper. According to Jal Mehta and Sarah Fine (2019), deeper learning is the understanding of not just the surface features of a subject or discipline but also the underlying structures or ideas. In their work visiting high schools across the country in search of deeper learning, they found that even in the most celebrated schools, the learning that allows students to grow as thinkers and critical and creative learners is more often the exception than the rule. Instead, they witnessed unchallenging instruction such as worksheets and tasks that were low level where students were expected to memorize content and apply algorithms rather than analyze, synthesize, and create.

In our practice, we have found that school and school system leaders sometimes consider their work around equity and culturally responsive practice as separate from deeper learning, whereas brilliant schools and school systems make the interconnectedness of equity and instructional excellence clear and coherent. In *Culturally Responsive Teaching and the Brain*, Zaretta Hammond (2015) creates a path forward for practitioners to engage in deeper learning themselves about the seamless interconnections:

> I don't see instructional equity merely in terms of system metrics like getting more kids into AP classes or advanced algebra. Because if we get more kids in advanced algebra, but they can't carry the cognitive load required for advanced algebra, that doesn't help anybody.
>
> When we think about equity as making sure every student reaches their intellectual capacity so they *can* carry a heavier cognitive load—so that they can take part in deep learning that is rigorous, for example—then we see how critical it is to create the kind of intellectual curiosity and engagement that allows us to kick-start students' information processing and meaning making. And I mean true intellectual engagement, not just having fun. Too often we reduce engagement to hands-on "activities" or to a lesson that's fun and interactive, but we don't

necessarily connect that interactivity to academic rigor or cognitive capacity building. And that's the thing that's so important. For me, the question is: *Do we do enough to create classroom environments for students to be intellectually curious?* The problem is not typically with the kids, who always come in with intellectual curiosity on some level. It's with the environments we are creating.

So, what shifts do educational leaders need to make to ensure that brilliant schools hold themselves accountable to a vision for deeper learning—one that implicates every school and system leader not only to hold the vision but build the capacity of their teams to realize it? We posit that it is the leader's role to build the capacity of their teams to

- **Allow students to drive the change they wish to see.** Survey students about their interests (i.e., academic topics) at the beginning of the year and/or before launching a new unit, and support teachers to be responsive to what they learn. Find, assess, and monitor progress of that change as you go.

- **Model a learning stance, ensuring that students know they do not have to have all the answers.** In this process, let students figure out the problems they want to solve and engage in deep analysis, synthesis, and ideation to arrive at solutions.

- **Engage in design thinking as a community.** Create content-related questions and discuss content about a student-identified problem of practice, and hold the adults accountable for building their own capacity to address those needs in nuanced ways.

- **Lead psychologically safe environments.** Encourage students to engage in learning processes to understand power structures and identify ways to question and challenge the school, district, community, and society at large.

- **Be deliberately developmental.** Create meaningful professional learning communities that maintain a deliberately developmental learning organization for every single member of the learning community, and challenge them to learn and adjust based on the ever-changing world.

Example 1: Leading with Values, Even If It Means Going Against the Grain

Cultivate a school or school system that stays focused on its vision for success and is willing to collectively stand by its values.

One example is having a process to uncover beliefs and state and local policies and to identify ways to advance the work despite backlash. Jeannie Stone, an outspoken and courageous Texas superintendent, was clear about the need to address inequities in Richardson Independent School District throughout her tenure. During Stone's five-year tenure, the district created a Department of Equity, Diversity, and Inclusion and an official equity policy. Stone oversaw work to tackle persistent racism, such as policies restricting access to gifted and talented classes. She took on conversations and asked her community to hold her accountable.

Example 2: Leverage "Internal" Accountability

Cultivate a school or school system that does not rely on external measures, standardized assessments, and/or entities to determine standards of success.

School and school systems should intentionally look inward as a regular part of practice. First, they hold one another accountable by examining their own performance, identifying unhelpful patterns in relation to expected outcomes. Elsie Rodriguez, superintendent of Monroe-Woodbury Central School District in Monroe, New York, is the vision setter for her district. She regularly engages her leadership team in reflective sessions to gauge their performance against the district's vision. Throughout the school year, they give one another performance feedback so that areas of improvement are explicitly named. District leaders in Monroe-Woodbury are aware of the team's performance and how to improve collectively and individually. In New York City, under former chancellor Meisha Porter's leadership, all divisions across the city were expected to work together to create a coherent approach for supporting 1,800 schools. Stepping into the seat in March 2020, Porter said, "As a principal, superintendent, and executive superintendent, I heard multiple messages from multiple divisions. The expectation is one team, one message." The deputy chancellors then worked together to bridge system-level initiatives into one coherent approach and held themselves accountable to ensuring everything they implemented from that point forward was communicated as one team and one approach.

Example 3: Teaming as a Driver

Cultivate a school or school system that leverages teaming to create a culture of feedback and high expectations.

These systems deeply invest in improving every adult's practice, ensuring high expectations with strong support and commitment to team success as a driver for improving student achievement. For example, engage in peer-to-peer feedback structures that do not shy away from difficult conversations about underperformance because they have created a culture where feedback is valued and intended to help adults grow and develop. In Baltimore City Schools, CEO Sonja Santelises has been steadfast in her belief that excellence in urban education is achievable at scale. "Our students have the same capacity for success as any other students. We must communicate and demonstrate our complete confidence in that capacity, by charting a pathway to success for each individual child. The real challenge is ours—as educators—to hold ourselves and our students accountable for their achievement" (Santelises, 2021, para. 5). Brilliant schools and school systems focus on the collective versus the individual. They know that nothing is possible without one another.

Example 4: Students as Designers of Deeper Learning

Cultivate a school or school system where students drive learning.

As a network, Big Picture Learning schools create conditions where students live lives by their own design. It may sound like hyperbole, but at Big Picture Learning, adults serve as caring facilitators and mentors. Each student at a Big Picture Learning school is part of a small learning community of 15 students called an advisory. Each advisory is supported and led by an advisor, a teacher who works closely with the group of students and forms personalized relationships with each advisee to identify interests and personalize learning accordingly. Having the student as the center of learning truly engages and challenges students and makes learning authentic and relevant. In addition, each student has an internship working closely with a mentor, learning in a real-world setting. Parents and families are actively involved in the learning process, helping to shape the student's learning plan, and are enrolled as resources to the school community. The result is a student-centered learning design, where students are actively invested in their learning and are challenged to pursue their interests by a supportive community of educators, professionals, and family members.

This learning model received national recognition from President Barack Obama for its innovative, personalized education program.

Example 5: Reciprocal Accountability

Cultivate a school or school system that centers on continuous improvement to better its practice.

As a principal and superintendent, Roberto understood that the most effective teachers have a deep knowledge of their content area, but they also have a deep knowledge of their students as individual learners. These teachers differentiate their instruction according to learning standards irrespective of a child's starting place with the ideology that students are the masters of their craft. The same is true for principals. The most effective principals know their teachers as individual learners, and superintendents and principal supervisors know their principals as individual learners. The primary accountability measure centers on vigilant teachers and leaders willing to improve their daily practice. Reciprocal accountability implicates every adult and establishes a through line connecting student learning to school improvement to professional learning needs.

In an effort to eliminate persistent academic disparities among Black and Latino boys, Roberto and his team participated in professional learning with teachers as learners so his team could tailor support accordingly. He did not focus on sanctions and rewards, but rather established an accountability culture for instructional improvement where teachers and leaders had the required knowledge and skills to hold themselves reciprocally accountable to student outcomes. *Accountability* was not a dirty word; rather, it was the impetus that drove teams to exceed expectations.

Now What?

Knowing how to address these systemic issues, educators, in every role in every classroom and across the school system, must take matters into their own hands. This will include actively defying ideologies around "saving" students of color in their classrooms who show potential. It calls on them to actively stop saying harmful things such as "If I can change just one child's life, . . ." which frees them of accountability for every other child they have the responsibility to serve. Every single adult is responsible for every single student. We must collectively own this notion. We have two options:

- We can make sure every single school, in every single neighborhood, is brilliant and
  - Innovative,
  - Asset based,
  - Community rich, and
  - Accountable to a vision for deeper learning.

Or

- We can continue doing what has perpetually harmed communities, find a few unicorns, and tell those students to leave to succeed.

Perpetuating the L2S mindset reveals who has the power in communities of color, who is worth saving, and who qualifies as knowledge bearers. Above all else, meritocracy is not the goal. Communities who determine who is good enough and who is not create a filtering system that has long plagued our nation to its fullest potential of becoming a country that works for everyone. So why are good people complicit? Because they have not regulated the dominant narrative about communities of color. They have succumbed to an ideology of tokenism or ableism. They believe that some children are unicorns rather than recognizing the genius and worth in each child. And those beliefs show up every single day in the interaction of school, student, and content.

To turn our vision into reality, leaders have to be highly skilled and incredibly intentional in their application of the counternarrative in action. If you want to raise your students' expectations of themselves, then simultaneously raise your expectations of yourself, too. Recognize their assets. Integrate into their community. Let innovation drive your path forward. And be accountable to the deeper learning of every single student.

SHOULDER UP

1. When you think about brilliant schools and classrooms for your own child, what do you envision? What do you want them to experience? What do you not want them not to experience? Identify the gap between what you want for your own child (or children you love) and what your system is providing to your students—then close that gap.

2. What are the trade-offs to leaving to succeed? How do we heal from the harm caused to students of color in an effort to attend "good" schools? When making recommendations to students about leaving the community, examine both the intended and unintended consequences of that decision with families. Be sure families and students are fully aware of the trade-offs.

3. What are the sacrifices we ask our families to make when their children attend schools that are inadequately prepared to support their growth and achievement? How do you hold to your promise of success for other people's children? How can you partner with the community in a way that disrupts cycles of harm? Meet with families regularly (not as tokens) to ensure their voices are consistently and respectfully included in your strategies for improvements.

4. How can you explicitly implicate every single adult in the school and system to ensure schools are innovative, asset based, community rich, and focused on deeper learning? How do your classrooms and schools support students to expand kids' view of possibilities for their learning and their life? Call yourself to action on one strategy in this chapter, and ask a colleague to observe your practice in real time and give you feedback.

Homegrown Leadership: Partnering with the Community to Disrupt the Dominant Narrative

The most powerful person in the world is the storyteller.

—Steve Jobs—

We task leaders with enormous responsibilities, including owning the work of disrupting long-held, harmful education practices. The truth is that leaders cannot do that intense kind of meaningful and impactful work absent of our families and communities. As the old adage from differently abled activists goes, "Nothing for us without us." So, how do leaders do this well? This chapter describes what it means to engage and partner with the community in meaningful ways, as well as the implications of rising up from within the community and coming in from the outside to lead in a home that isn't yours.

Regardless of a leader's status as an insider or outsider, the consistent narrative about low-income communities of color is deficit based and must be rewritten. If not, educators will likely continue to interact with students and families through a deficit lens and perpetuate not only the harm to our communities but also the continued distrust and tension between leaders and the communities they serve.

We have consistently shared examples of the greatness that exists in our communities. Our convictions are indeed a result of our own personal experiences as well as learning from other extraordinary, often-unseen leaders who espoused similar stories. We believe in elevating more stories of triumph and greatness. How do we as leaders empower individuals within the communities we serve to tell their own stories? How do you tell a story you don't know firsthand or own? How do leaders strategically help rewrite the narrative and expose the beauty that has been hidden from the public? Of course, the question about who does the storytelling remains an important consideration. There are three ways to think about storytelling in this context:

- What stories we tell;
- How we create the opportunities and structures for others to share and hear those stories; and
- How we leverage storytelling as a key lever to disrupt harmful narratives and tell the stories that reflect the beauty of communities we serve.

Indeed, to disrupt the leave to succeed mindset, we need to think critically about the stories we tell and create community partnerships grounded in trust. Trust has always been and must remain the foundation. We must also be willing to make bold leadership moves that call out harm and inspire a vision forward.

And we must acknowledge that being a homegrown leader or a leader with a track record who enters the community does not automatically grant you the authority to tell the community's story—it is an honor you must earn and then work to keep. Building trusting relationships and the credibility to speak on behalf of those you serve is indeed a privilege that must be curated and maintained.

Intended and Unintended Consequences of Homegrown Leadership

Returning to work in one's community is all about heart and soul—having the heart to be intentional and courageous with enough soul to be emphatic in serving the community faithfully. In doing so, it is often difficult to separate the "work" from your personal mission and experiences in the community. Not only are you surrounded by memories of the way this community personally impacted your life, but the expectations of your contribution as a leader are different from those of an outsider.

As former Chicago Schools CEO Janice Jackson noted:

> Leading a school district that you came up through is a huge benefit because you know everyone, and they know you. But there is also an immense amount of pressure because people know you and your credibility. They know your history and the experiences that bond you to them. If I were the leader in a place that didn't know me, expectations might not be as high. In a place where they know you and they know you understand the experience, they expect more.

Similarly, former Denver Public Schools superintendent Susana Cordova shared, "Being from the community and having worked there for 30-plus years, I felt really proud and really frustrated. On one hand, I know how hard we fought for all the gains we made. At the same time, the impact of slow and steady progress isn't fast enough. When you are from the place you are leading, the work is very, very personal." Through Cordova's lived experiences as a superintendent, she was constantly reminded that being one of the few representatives of the community leaves little room for error.

> These words run through your daily thoughts and you set a huge burden of expectations on your own shoulders.
> - "I cannot make a mistake."
> - "I need to do right by my community."
> - "I need to be the leader our community has long-needed."

- "All eyes are on me."
- "Can I really do this?"

In Roberto's case, in his first week as superintendent, he drove by various locations where he once lived. Location after location presented a visual reminder of the many times his family was uprooted, evicted, and forced to move. He recalled many painful memories from his upbringing that were unavoidable. In the blink of an eye, these memories flooded his conscience. Suddenly he began encountering people who were either part of his past or knew of it.

In Nancy's case, she would become the school principal and supervisor of teachers who had mistreated and miseducated her siblings and other family members. She would walk the school campus where her mother had recounted some of her most painful experiences growing up. Now, Nancy was in charge and was expected to confront these wrongs.

Home was staring them both in the face, and there was no avoiding it.

The associations with your upbringing look different for different leaders. Take Veronica Crespin-Palmer for example, the co-founder and lead executive officer of RISE Colorado.

Vignette 4.1: From Colorado to East LA and Back
CEO Veronica Crespin-Palmer

Veronica Crespin-Palmer would return to her childhood home in Colorado to found RISE—an experience that was as beautiful as it was painful. RISE Colorado is an organization that works to educate, engage, and empower low-income families and families of color to rise as change agents for educational equity in our public school system. Although she had returned home, she surprisingly felt more at home in her previous experience teaching and leading in Los Angeles, where she had felt seen and acknowledged.

How could it not be? Los Angeles is the home of rich Chicano/Latino history, from the East LA walkouts, to Garfield High School's famous Bolivian American calculus teacher Jaime Escalante, to the larger Chicano movement where Mexican Americans developed a political consciousness and greater sense of ethnic solidarity, acknowledging their "subordinate" status in American society and developing a collective determination to act.

When Crespin-Palmer went back to Colorado to bring her knowledge and gifts to the community that had raised her, founding RISE along with three other Latinas from the neighborhood, it was a struggle to get the larger community to believe in and fund their work. This caused Crespin-Palmer and her colleagues to use their own money and make personal sacrifices on behalf of the work. "Although we were Latina co-founders from the community, we were still told that we had to prove ourselves."

Meanwhile, white male outsiders were getting funded with ease, backed by various groups to launch their idea to support her community. The pain associated with rejection from her home community was even more difficult than it would have been elsewhere. Still, she and her co-founders persisted.

Veronica got inspired in Los Angeles to create change in her home community, but not without deep personal sacrifice.

Indeed, we are often called to the stage to share our successes. What we rarely share, however, are the real-life experiences of our family and friends who were negatively affected by the school system. Often, in trying to keep our community motivated (internally) or save face for our community (externally) and to avoid further judgment, we have avoided some of the truth and pain that continue to linger today. Instead, we share our stories of survivorship. This internal battle reflects a constant conflict to either do what is right by being a voice for our community (and communities like ours) or hold our community and the systems that have plagued it accountable. At times, doing what is right is not clear.

The return home, though one of celebration, means that you give up much of the anonymity leaders often desire. For example, a leader may choose to live outside the neighborhood they work in in order to separate the professional from personal. Similarly, privacy or anonymity is lost when others know you beyond your résumé; they usually know your family's history, your academic and personal history in schools, and other pieces of your life. They know these things about you because they are things that have defined them, too. These symbiotic experiences are analogous to the workplace. Leaders who understand this can achieve some early wins in their tenure.

Yet, the stakes as well as the pressure of having and protecting the seat you hold are high. When you do make a mistake, the criticism is often fierce and sometimes unforgiving—especially from your own people.

Former Chicago Public Schools CEO Janice Jackson continues to live in the community today. "It is uncommon that people see the leader of their school system at church, at the grocery store, the gym, or the salon. I am very much a part of the community. I live among the people who I serve. I am always serving my community."

In fact, it is even more difficult to separate work from your person because you are "always on." The community will look to you for answers and expect you to be responsive even during downtime or off hours. If you set boundaries, you will have to do so with great care. Boundaries are important to set for your personal freedom but cannot be at the expense of the community's critique that you are not "all in." It is a careful navigation. Work and personal life become intertwined and the level of deep commitment to the community is different from deep commitment to a job. After all, this is *home*.

Although we do believe in coming home to give back and we want you to encourage our youth that doing so is a viable option, we also remind you that after you receive a standing ovation, you will need to roll up your sleeves and lean into the work in ways that are deeply personal.

Leading a Community That Isn't Yours . . . Yet

When you lead as an outsider, you have the moral responsibility to learn about the context you intend to serve.

The question then becomes, what makes for an "outsider"? What if you grew up in a community with similar demographics and cultural practices? What if you have served the same community for years? Or what if you grew up in the community and then left to succeed but returned to give back?

An illustrative example is Newark's mayoral race of 2014—a race by two "insiders" who would be charged with confronting complex community challenges. At the time, Newark had its highest murder rate in two decades, the state was threatening to take over the city's troubled finances, and the school system had been run and failed by the state for two decades. And although both candidates were from Newark, the community perceived them as very different leaders and contributors. Both candidates shared their plans for turning the city and school system around.

Vignette 4.2: Newark Mayoral Race 2014
Ras Baraka and Shavar Jeffries

In 2014, Newark's mayoral race was between two people from Newark's South Ward: Ras Baraka and Shavar Jeffries. Mayor Ras Baraka would ultimately win with more than 53 percent of the vote and 87 percent of precincts reporting (Pizarro, 2014).

Baraka had made his name as a community organizer, a public school teacher, the principal of Central High School, and a city council member, positioning himself as a champion of the underserved. He drew on his father Amiri Baraka's fiery legacy as well as his own talent, promising to "take Newark back" from corporate interests. Besides union and longtime community activists, supporters included dozens of Baraka's former students from Central High School who said that they had worked throughout the campaign "to support my principal."

The interesting part about the race was who Baraka was running against: former assistant state attorney general Shavar Jeffries, who was also from Newark's South Ward and had dedicated his life to civil rights and social justice.

Jeffries, born to a teenage mother who was murdered when he was 10, was raised by his grandmother in Newark, where a school counselor at the local Boys and Girls Club helped get him a scholarship to an elite suburban prep school. He would then attend Duke University and Columbia Law School and return to Newark as a public school teacher and civil rights attorney. He also helped to found a network of charter schools and became president of the district school board (Pizarro, 2014). The teacher's union president at the time still said, "The people of Newark are looking for a leader that defies the establishment." Although Jeffries was a Newark native who had left to develop himself and then returned to give back, the comment suggested that many considered him an outsider.

This story brings about several questions about what it means to be "from the community" and whether there are consequences associated with leaving home to build yourself and then returning to lead only to be seen as "the other." Are we, who leave and return, seen as an outsider or a person who no longer stands in solidarity with our community? Is it even our community anymore?

The community plays an important role in shaping the narrative. Often, these leadership experiences play out publicly, and questions about who is deserving of the community's trust and respect come into play. Work around building trust is key to any leader, whether insider or outsider.

So What? Now What?

The complexity of this work requires very intentional and deliberate moves to build trust and explicitly disrupt the deficit-based dominant narratives that have plagued our communities for centuries. Leaders must shift their daily personal practices as well as the systemic practices of schools to an asset-based, community-centered approach. To do so, it requires leaders to

1. Look to the community for answers to collective pain;
2. Transparently acknowledge and own sins from the past;
3. Actively combat mistrust while rebuilding partnership;
4. Balance leadership with community ownership of the vision; and
5. Rewrite the narrative together.

1. Look to the Community for Answers to Collective Pain

Do our communities look inside for answers or outside? Do outsiders think it is their role to arrive in our communities with silver bullets and answers to our most persistent challenges? The superhero myth is dangerous because it perpetuates the leave to succeed mindset. In this schema, the superhero from the outside has more expertise than those who live in the community. Or, the superhero represents one of the few who were by some sort of miracle "rescued" from a poor, dangerous, and hopeless community and have returned to save the day. This long-held schema reinforces the deficit narrative and presents our communities through what Adiche (2009) calls a "single story" with no mention of efforts by everyday community members who have become teachers, organizers, parents, and leaders in their own right, working as a collective to overcome systemic neglect.

Geoffrey Canada, former president of the Harlem Children's Zone, dispelled the urban myth that someone will come and save the day. This superhero fallacy was theatrically featured on the big screen in *Waiting for Superman* in 2010. In this grim public education documentary, Canada recounts his childhood experience in New York City schools and the decision to live with his grandparents in a suburban school district on Long Island. He shares, "At 9 years old, I realized that I wanted to come back and help kids like those of us growing up in these conditions. Every class I took in high school from that point forward was really in preparation for trying to come back and make a difference with children in poor communities."

Children, families, and communities have the right to be disappointed if they are "waiting for Superman." The superhero myth does not reflect the reality that resources matter, poverty matters, and access to effective teachers and leaders matters. However, anyone who returns home to transform their community or school system must first consider the human talent and leadership that already exists within as opposed to actively looking for superheroes.

And leaders exist with or without formal titles or degrees.

The 1982 film *Gandhi* depicting Mahatma Gandhi's journey includes a scene where he meets with British nationals and tells them that they are "masters in someone else's home," then asks them to leave India forever. The British argue that without their rule, India will likely tear itself apart. Gandhi retorts that although problems will certainly arise, they are India's problems, not Britain's.

In other words, the answer is in the room. We, as communities, have the solutions to our long-standing problems, not a superhero.

When former Denver superintendent Susana Cordova faced criticism as her appointment to superintendency was being considered in 2018, Landon Mascareñaz, then vice president for community partnership at the Colorado Education Initiative and a state board member for the Colorado Community College system, came to her defense. In a passionate piece in *The 74*, Mascareñaz wrote:

> Some of her opposition has come from the education reform community. Yet unlike many chicken-hawk reformers, she actually attended—or had family and friends who attended—many of the schools where she was asked to lead challenging change management conversations. How many of these self-proclaimed reformers have led tough community conversations in schools they once attended? How many have had to look their cousins and family friends in the eye and have a difficult discussion about how the district is not serving their school and community? Or about the imperfect options moving forward? Far from being a critique of Cordova, it is a sign of her public courage. (Mascareñaz, 2008, paras. 18–19)

Communities across the United States have the capacity and courage to solve the ills at their doorstep. Although leaders act as a conduit and facilitator of change, you can never do it in the absence of the community, regardless of your status as an insider or outsider.

Instead, it becomes essential to become what Shane Safir (2017b) calls a "listening leader" as both a skill and a mindset when partnering with communities to tackle the most persistent problems. In this context, the leader acts as a facilitator, guide, and extra set of eyes, as opposed to the know-it-all superhero. We can always learn knowledge and perspective from people around us. Active, intentional listening is a powerful tool to earn trust and build productive relationships. In this approach, the ability to listen and learn establishes a rapport with the community and builds trust to truly partner in collective progress.

2. Transparently Acknowledge and Own Sins from the Past

Regardless of whether or not you—yes, *you*—caused the harm in the community, you must humble yourself to acknowledge and own it.

Yet the "how" to acknowledge and own sins of the past is not a one-size-fits-all solution. This must be done within the comfort of a leader's own identity and preferred boundaries. At a minimum, you must have an answer to the crucial question "Are you part of the system or an advocate for the community? Where are your loyalties?" And the answer must be backed up with evidence based on actions, not just words. As Padilla (2019) put it, leaders must courageously shift from rhetoric to action. The assumption that a leader automatically gets a pass when they are from the community is a misnomer. In fact, as we've noted, it could be even more difficult.

Consider Caddo Parish superintendent T. Lamar Goree, who shared:

> When I returned back to the district, I was surprised at how much had changed and yet how much had not since I attended schools in Caddo Parish. The last schools built opened before I graduated and with that the buildings were aging and in desperate need of repair. More concerning was the community's perception of the school system and lack of faith in the ability of Caddo Parish to provide a high-quality education. From my first community meetings, there were discussions of what I refer to now as the "sins of the past" in which individuals were upset about issues which had nothing to do with myself, the teachers, or administrators. Yet we nonetheless had to work to change those feelings and move our district forward.

Goree was troubled by the challenges associated with his return. How could he be coupled with the sins of the past when he was returning to serve? But assuming a leadership role in and of itself carries the responsibility of reentering with a learning stance and a great deal of humility. You do not get to skip this step just because you are from the community. And you certainly do not get to skip this step as an outsider.

3. Actively Combat Mistrust While Rebuilding Partnership

In the complexity of representing the larger system that the community struggles to trust, we have found transparency around the active moves to build trusting partnerships to be key. Stakeholders need to understand the why or the purpose behind any and all decisions, even when they disagree with a decision. The biggest mistake you can make is not understanding the newfound power in your leadership role and assuming that you still hold the same influence and interactions you did when you lived in the community. Similarly, a big mistake for outsiders is assuming that an impressive résumé or set of experiences will continue to win them credibility. As Nancy's Harvard doctoral advisor Robert Kegan says, "Your résumé will last 15 minutes. Your impact will depend on how you interact, engage, and treat people." At the end of the day, you are now the "formal" leader, and whether you are from the community or an outsider to it, questions will emerge.

Truly, for us authors, it didn't matter that we were from the community—and the formal title we had recently earned only got us "in the door." There were three crucial prerequisites to earning our communities' trust. First, we had to humble ourselves with the understanding that communities shift over time and that the community we once knew no longer existed in the same way. Second, we had to own and appreciate that the answers to any problems existed within the community and that change needed to happen with, not to, stakeholders. Lastly, we had to recognize that there was a lot of damage to undo, and whether we liked it or not, we were now formal representatives of the problem. As leaders, we were part of the formal group who had done that damage over time. Rebuilding trust was key to our success as leaders. We were acutely aware of the questions many in our communities had:

- Can we trust her?
- Is he trying to take advantage of our community to make a name for himself?
- What are their intentions?

It is tempting to fall into conversations where you, as a formal leader of the community, are being highlighted as the one who "made it." Though it is true that you have achieved a level of success that allows you to lead in an official role, you have to leverage language that allows you to own your newfound responsibilities while disrupting the idea that you are an exception to the rule and somehow more "special" than the community itself. The one thing that is true is that you are an example of the potential of every young person in the community.

Even if you think you know the community, commit to rediscovering it—learn about the various experiences that existed beyond your own history that share your understanding of its beauty and struggles. If this is your home community, this step includes admitting that you may not know your old community even when you grew up in it. Maybe part of that authenticity is the vulnerability of admitting what you don't know and the willingness to learn about how your hometown or the neighborhood you are entering has evolved over time.

One powerful strategy involves, again, listening, but in this case, repeat what you hear back to those who are willing to share with you to ensure you have actually heard what they are trying to convey. This gives the speaker a chance to clarify anything if necessary. Reflective listening, a practice at the center of Carl Rogers's empathy approach, involves seeking to understand another person's ideas or thoughts and then offering the idea back to the speaker to confirm your understanding. As part of this process, it is important to acknowledge the power and authority you bring to the table.

As superintendent of several large school districts, Richard Carranza would say at the start of a learning experience, "I ask every single one of you, myself included, to put our titles to the side and enter the room as learners." This gives the leader the opportunity to get to know their communities beyond typical surface-level types of activities but instead based on real stories and real relationships. These stories and relationships then can be seamlessly integrated into a shared, co-owned vision for success, grounded in a collective why, and then translated into a snowball effect that scales trust and partnership.

4. Balancing Your Leadership with Community Ownership of the Vision

Who owns the vision is critical. Even when you return "home" to lead your community, it is imperative that you lead through collective ownership of the challenges ahead. We are adamantly against the one-person show.

Leadership works when the community owns it, not when one person or one small team owns it. If the intent of your leadership is the clichéd "If I can influence one child, . . ." then you don't need the community by your side—and by the way, don't lead in our neighborhoods. Influencing one young person equals mentorship, so become a Big Brother or Big Sister. Assuming your leadership envisions creating positive and sustainable change for an entire community, you need the collective. Take the experience of the late Nipsey Hussle, born Ermias Asghedom, for example.

Vignette 4.3: Community Ownership as the Antidote
Nipsey Hussle's Vision

Nipsey, an American rapper, entrepreneur, and community activist who started off rapping on the streets of Los Angeles and could have easily left the community with his newfound wealth, instead focused on using his success to rebuild Crenshaw (Frank, 2019). He bought a neighborhood burger restaurant, a fish market, and a barbershop. He donated shoes to every student at 59th Street Elementary School and financed improvements on their playground, including basketball courts. He employed countless neighborhood residents. He worked to empower and employ his community through real estate investments, as well as science and tech learning centers for teens.

In 2019, just two months before he died, he closed escrow on the shopping plaza that housed his Marathon store, with plans to build a 100-unit residential building on the property—the same place he was shot and killed.

Nipsey Hussle's work was just in its beginning stages. We don't know what would have ultimately happened, but his theory of action was that investing in the community required share ownership of those directly impacted (Reed, 2021).

In fact, one key lesson we both learned returning to our community was that our success was meaningless without a direct effort to lift a community of people. In Nipsey Hussle's example, there were unintended consequences to his reinvestment and perhaps a different expectation than an outsider who had invested in the same way. Although his vision was for the community to own the vision, that commitment requires time and careful navigation of stakeholders. Insiders may see your efforts as disingenuous, and outsiders may see them as a threat. Although all of our efforts are well intended, the impact may be experienced differently by stakeholders. This is why it is critical to be inclusive of the processes and decision making as you lead.

As Harry Spence, former commissioner of the Massachusetts Department of Social Services and former Harvard Professor of Practice, says, "People don't resist change; they resist being the object of others' change agenda."

Thus, community ownership of a vision requires the community to be inspired by the vision, participate in it, and feel its direct impact on their own life and the lives of people they love. Process always takes more time, but as the African proverb says, "If you want to go fast, go alone. If you want to go far, go together."

5. Rewrite the Narrative Together

Just as indigenous communities have relied on stories, leaders anywhere can leverage storytelling to make connections, change mindsets, transmit culture, build community, and change the narrative. Many frameworks have been established to help us do that.

One of our favorites is Harvard Kennedy School professor Marshall Ganz's Public Narrative framework: *Story of Self, Us, and Now*. According to Ganz (2012), "Stories communicate our values through the language of the heart. From stories we learn how to manage ourselves, how to face difficult choices, unfamiliar situations and uncertain outcomes because each of us is the protagonist in our own life story, facing everyday challenges, authoring our own choices, and learning from the outcomes."

Ganz was introduced to storytelling through the practice of organizing. In 1964, he dropped out of Harvard College to volunteer for the Mississippi Summer Project during the civil rights movement and worked in a freedom house in McComb. Following this experience, he worked alongside Cesar Chavez and the United Farm Workers for 16 years in California. Throughout these experiences, he leveraged structured (two- to five-minute) storytelling as a key strategy to mobilize stakeholders to action. His framework includes three types of stories:

- **Story of self:** A simple story that connects the audience to why you were personally called to the work.
- **Story of us:** A shared story connecting the audience to shared purpose, shared goals, and a shared vision.
- **Story of now:** A call to action that surfaces the challenge the community faces, the choices it must make, and the hope to which the community can aspire.

Widely recognized across many sectors, the Public Narrative framework has helped many to build bridges across differences, from leaders hoping to be elected president of the United States to those hoping to become school superintendents. Leveraging this model can support a community in rewriting its narrative. Here are our own examples:

Vignette 4.4: "I cannot wait to be your teacher!"
Nancy's Public Narrative

> **Story of Self:** It was 1992, the beginning of my 8th grade year at a large middle school in East San Jose. I was excited about seeing my friends but had no interest in meeting my new teachers. My family's negative experiences in schools over the years had created a distrust for teachers—and principals, for that matter.

At 13 years old, I felt like I was in a perpetual game of tug-of-war with my teachers in addition to the tug-of-war between the school and my mother, between our low-income community and its institutional saviors trying to "help" all of us Mexican American kids "get out of the barrio." I was aware of the way people referred to our schools as "low-performing" and "dangerous."

But on this day in 1992, I walked into Mr. Lovelace's classroom to start my first day of 8th grade. He was a tall white man in his early 30s with reddish-brown curly hair and blue eyes. I remember staring up at his white collared shirt and tie. Sure, he was white like the rest of 'em, but there was something different about the way he welcomed me into his classroom. He didn't give me an immediate "I am the boss" attitude. He simply said hello with a genuine smile and added, "I am so excited to have you in my class! I was your sister's teacher two years ago, so I've visited your home and have tried your mother's enchiladas! I cannot wait to be your teacher!"

I had never experienced anything like that before—teachers typically didn't want me in their classes. Not only did Mr. Lovelace seem to want me there, but he also created such an interesting learning experience. He threw out the textbook and engaged us in discussions about current events and popular music, and he even introduced us to authors of color like Maya Angelou! I still remember when our class broke down the lyrics of Tracy Chapman's song "Fast Car." Mr. Lovelace's classroom became my sanctuary, and for two hours every school day, I allowed myself to submit to the institution. It could have my attention. My time. My respect. And it could even have a little bit of my vulnerability, at least when I was in Mr. Lovelace's class.

Story of Us: But many of my friends and siblings didn't get lucky enough to land in a classroom like Mr. Lovelace's. And I know many of you reading this story and other children across our country, in particular from low-income communities of color, didn't have the same chance or experience to feel seen, validated, and rigorously challenged the way I did in his class.

Story of Now: What would it take to make sure every single classroom on a school campus creates meaningful, relevant, and culturally affirming learning experiences for our young people?

I'm convinced that the answer is leadership.

Leadership has a multiplier effect—its impact is exponential because leaders have the ability to find, develop, and encourage culturally responsive teaching and learning like I experienced in Mr. Lovelace's classroom.

When we ensure that there is an exceptional leader in every school, we can ensure that classroom after classroom is filled with an exceptional teacher. And when we ensure that there are exceptional superintendents at the helm of every school system, we can ensure that school after school is filled with exceptional principals.

Join me to ensure that my experience with Mr. Lovelace in 8th grade is not an exception but the norm for every child, every classroom, every school, every school system—and in particular, in communities that have historically been excluded from this level of support and access.

Vignette 4.5: No Such Thing as Bootstraps
Roberto's Public Narrative

Story of Self: When I reflect on how my journey came to be, I can't help but think about bootstraps.

I grew up in Newburgh, a city once known as the murder capital of New York. As a result, there was not a choice—I had to acquire hard-knock-life credentials. According to many, I am the perfect example of the hard worker who pulled himself up and out of the place that would weigh him down, if he let it. "You just have to pull yourself up by your bootstraps!" they often say. But have you ever actually tried to pull yourself up by your bootstraps? Probably not, because it's impossible. Like many others, I am the story *of* my community, not *despite* my community.

Like so many of our country's male children of color, I was once deemed a likely dropout destined for a life of crime and poverty. But the murder of my two close friends in high school shook me awake and set me on a different path in life.

I didn't want to go down the same road as my fallen friends. So, at 15 years old, I moved out. As I had a rotation of couches I slept on, I ultimately was taken in by a close friend. For the first time, I went to class with a purpose. Very quickly, I experienced a different kind of attention and reaction from school personnel. Instead of getting kicked out of class, struggling with assignments, or responding to their low expectations, I showed up on time, completed my work, stayed after school, and asked for help. As a result, I started to experience school very differently. My efforts led to dramatically improved grades, honor roll status, and college options. Before this, I had soared on the football field and on the wrestling mat; however, I had never recognized my academic potential.

When I realized that my effort and nurturing home environment could lead to success, it was an absolute game changer. Sadly, what had led to this realization was a traumatic event. Truthfully, I am not sure why this particular trauma over many other traumas I had experienced changed my trajectory in life, but I know it should not have to be this way. It was because of this that I committed my life to education—my own and that of thousands of other children like me.

Story of Us: The beauty and potential that was within me is within all of our youth, and it shouldn't take a traumatic event for the people in our students' lives to notice. In some cases, having your friends murdered and/or in prison will wake you up, and for others, it will get you deeper into dysfunction. For me, it made me reach inside myself for something better.

But what if young people felt what I felt after losing my friends from the beginning? What if we could find and nurture that spirit in them? How would our communities feel and react if we blanketed them with love? If our interactions were more nurturing and reflective of high expectations, no matter what our students brought to us? What if we stopped writing off students based on their stories and instead recognized their potential and validated their greatness from day one—because of their stories?

This kind of leadership is definitely something that my friends, and many of you reading my story, would have benefited from throughout your schooling experience. And it is something that the students, and all long-underestimated communities of color, deserve today.

Story of Now: Communities like mine don't need bootstrap analogies. We need high expectations, nurturing environments, and forgiving adults. You never know when it's going to "click" for a child, so we cannot give up. Plus, we must shift our lens to seeing the many assets our youth bring to the table. Every child is a genius, and every child is worth loving and nurturing. My equity charge in educational leadership is not to allow the conditions of race, zip code, ethnicity, or language to be predictors for success in life.

Join me in personally investing in communities reflected in the book. Our students deserve nothing less.

Another framework for storytelling we have leveraged is the Storytelling Project at Barnard College. Bell and colleagues (2008) push us to distinguish the various types of stories and narratives we share and tell through a social justice lens. The project depicts four kinds of stories: stock stories, concealed stories, resistance stories, and emerging/transforming stories.

- **Stock stories:** A stock story is what you would find on a website or in common terminology, such as the American Dream. Stock stories often go unquestioned and are collectively maintained. Because they only brush the surface, they neutralize challenges and make reality invisible.

- **Concealed stories:** Concealed stories, on the other hand, shake up the status quo. They narrate the ways that varying experiences, and specifically race, shape experiences and opportunities. It takes work and effort to uncover concealed stories.

- **Resistance stories:** Resistance stories emerge from concealed stories when they are documented, told, or passed down. They are stories about leaders who challenged racism, such as the full story of Rosa Parks that includes the organized collective planning of many people, not just the actions of one brave woman. Or the story of Dolores Huerta, who coined the famous slogan *sí, se puede* ("yes, we can"), which inspired President Obama's own campaign battle cry and has often wrongly been attributed to Cesar Chavez. Or civil rights activist and prominent leader Ella Baker, without whom Dr. King's work—and the civil rights movement of the 1960s—may not have succeeded. These stories have the potential to inspire and mobilize people.

- **Emerging stories:** Emerging stories tell the experiences of people in the present and the different ways that they, in their lives, reimagine categories, boundaries, and relationships. Emerging stories have not yet been heard and help to reshape current narratives of time and place.

In our L2S resistance story, educators would encourage and create systems that reward students who return to their community to give back. For example, in the Brockton Public Schools system in Massachusetts, the district created incentives to invite students to return to the community to teach. The same is happening in Chicago, Illinois; Buffalo, New York; Austin, Texas; Yonkers, New York; and so many other school systems. District leaders are creating opportunities for community members to be change makers, to serve the communities they love and to build the communities they want.

Taking control of and shaping the narrative helps us shift the deficit-based story from "all the things that have gone wrong" to a space to imagine all the things that we are responsible for redefining and renaming. And the beautiful thing about that is that so many amazing but unheard and invisible stories already exist. It is a leader's job to tell them.

Storytelling, in multiple forms and as part of consistent day-to-day interactions, have the potential to shift the leave to succeed narrative.

Closing

Coming home is a true gift—and it can also be a curse. While many outsiders enter majority-minority communities looking to share their gifts and get applauded for helping "communities in need," some of us, despite the advice to never return, simply come home. Returning home is humbling, not only because going to "work" becomes very personal, but also because your community can sometimes be even harder on you than on an outsider making their way in to help.

There is nothing inherently wrong with leaving your community to succeed in order to pursue learning or career opportunities. Both of us left home, but we did so with a firm understanding that our communities were not defective. We left with an appreciation that whatever fruit we bore was only possible because of our roots. The struggles we lived through in our communities made us who we are. However, when we returned home to share the fruits of our labor with our home communities, our role as education leaders was more complicated than we had thought. Though we were once insiders, we had become outsiders and had to re-earn our street cred.

Does the beauty outweigh the struggle? We say, yes, every time.

It is a true badge of honor. And one that must be encouraged and applauded.

As we see in examples of communities such as East Los Angeles, it is important to change the narrative and share the stories of pride in identity and struggle that make coming home an amazing example of the ultimate "success." And if you are an outsider to the community, you have the responsibility to do the necessary work to earn the privilege and honor to share the stories of the community members you serve in a way that they anoint versus only through your lens.

SHOULDER UP

1. When you think of the community you serve, how do you describe it? Talk to a community member. Describe their community in your own words and have them give you warm and cool feedback.

2. When you think of the successes you have had on behalf of the community you've led, how do you tell the story? Give the authors credit for their work. When opportunities arise to share community stories and successes publicly, invite the authors and the architects.

3. How will you create spaces for more storytelling, both within and across communities? Locate current venues/platforms/locations in the community that are used as safe spaces where stories originate. Teach various storytelling frameworks and allow community members to find and elevate their voices.

4. Whether an insider or outsider to the community, how do you elevate various community members and leaders across the community? Identify the people and the stories that lift communities without ignoring the most significant pain points. Elevate community leadership at every opportunity.

Redefining Success

If you have come to help me, you are wasting your time.
But if you have come because your liberation
is bound up with mine, then let us walk.

—Lila Watson—

An asset-based approach to educating students in America's classrooms is the key to achieving equity. However, it requires redefining success. The act of redefining success is the responsibility of the leader to ensure that everyone in their community believes that all children, especially historically marginalized children, are able to achieve the highest levels. The work of redefining success through an asset-based mindset cannot be done in absence of leadership.

Researchers Leithwood and colleagues (2004, 2010) found that leadership is second only to classroom instruction among all school-related factors that contribute to student achievement. Furthermore, they found that demonstrated effects of successful leadership are considerably greater in schools that are in more difficult circumstances. In 2021, the Wallace

Foundation commissioned research to update these findings, concluding that the principal is as important as the teacher and has greater impact and magnitude (Grissom et al., 2021). The study also indicated the critical importance of continued reorientation toward education equity.

In considering what is required to disrupt the leave to succeed mindset and other deficit-based mindsets that live in our schools, classrooms, and communities, it is clear that leadership, for education equity, matters.

In advancing this work, leaders, at both the school and systems levels, must make the choice to exemplify what it means to lead for equity. One way they can do this is by modeling what it means to bring their full selves to the work in order to create the conditions for hope, change, and pride in self and community. An effective leader knows that the first step is with themselves. As Dufour (2004) suggests, leaders must "look in the mirror" instead of "out the mirror." He argues that leaders far too often focus on outward forces over which they have little control. Emdin (2016) noted in *For White Folks Who Teach in the Hood,* "The time will always come when teachers [leaders] must ask themselves if they will follow the mold or blaze a new trail. There are serious risks that come with this decision. It essentially boils down to whether one chooses to do damage to the system or the student."

In leadership, this decision comes with political implications depending on the authorizing environment in which you're entering or reentering. Blaming poverty to justify current practices or low achievement is a tempting phenomenon because it absolves the leader and the community from the responsibility of taking action and owning the change they wish to see. When engaged in this work, leaders either stay the course or take an "off ramp" when opposition presents itself. Which path will you choose?

We ask leaders to hold up a mirror and look at how their leadership will disrupt deficit mindsets so they can infuse an asset-based mindset across the entire system they are charged to lead. Reflect on these questions:

- How do your day-to-day leadership moves advance an asset-based culture of success, and where do they reinforce deficit-based mindsets?

- How do the actions, decisions, and the policies you promote substantiate a narrow definition of success?

We believe that the answers to most complex questions and what seem like the most intractable problems lie in leadership's sphere of influence. Though we do not believe leaders are superheroes, we do believe, as the 2021 Wallace-commissioned study found, that leaders have an exponential impact and significant responsibility to redefine success from an asset-based frame. Leaders play a crucial role in reshaping the future.

The question then becomes how success is defined and whether leaders have the courage to recognize the many assets that exist within the communities they serve. These leaders, in collaboration with stakeholders, forge a new, shared path to this definition.

Six Leadership Moves That Can Redefine Success

After interviewing several successful leaders across the country, we identified six explicit moves that, when done well, have the potential to set the conditions needed to redefine success from an asset-based frame and with the understanding that receiving the formal role and title does not equal leadership. Leadership is a deliberate choice and requires day-to-day intentionality.

1. Model authenticity.
2. Call out in order to call in.
3. Tackle beliefs.
4. Differentiate between investment in community and investment in ego.
5. Lead from behind the eyes.
6. Activate the counternarrative.

Model Authenticity

Modeling authenticity means bringing your full self to the table. It requires comfort in naming your blind spots and vulnerabilities, as well as your thinking and your perspective. Professor Mark Moore at the

John F. Kennedy School of Government at Harvard University regularly says that your ideas are not real until you make them public. Share your truth. Share your perspective. This requires exceptional courage and vulnerability and is one of the most powerful tools you possess. As you model this, others will follow, particularly as you deliberately make spaces for others to show up in their truth. Elevating voices of those commonly unheard allows every person in the community to be celebrated for the skin they are in and for the unique talents they bring.

Vignette 5.1: "I Have to Be Me"
Former Chancellor Richard Carranza

"I have transitioned into five new communities since teaching and leading in my hometown of Tucson, Arizona." Though the new communities Carranza entered, including San Francisco, Houston, and New York City, were not his original home, they represented an extended version of it. They served communities he cared about deeply, and upon entering, he needed these communities to know he was there to listen and learn. He also understood that, although he could add tremendous value and expertise, the communities knew their context best. In these homes, Carranza did his best to listen, learn, and respect others' voices and experiences.

"I've learned to enter new communities the same way I was taught by my parents to enter new rooms. They raised me to never put on airs—to greet every single person in the space and respect every home you enter." Communities are homes.

In this work, Carranza brings his full self, each and every time. When he was announced as superintendent of the Houston Independent School District, he greeted his new community by singing "El Rey," a composition by José Alfredo Jiménez, alongside the Northside High School Mariachis. He has continued to bring that aspect of his identity as well as his family's story into every new community. Carranza says, "Sometimes who I am will connect with others and sometimes it won't. But I have to be me. If I bring the vulnerability of my full self into the context and I engage in deeper listening, then it affords me the opportunity to transparently share what I see and let that sync up with my why. Sometimes my why syncs up and sometimes it doesn't."

Throughout Carranza's tenure as the chancellor of the New York City DOE, he consistently shared his deep love for the Bronx: "If I was from New York City, I would've been born in the Bronx. It reminds me of home." Home, thus, does not have to be one's actual hometown but a place that represents it. In all of these settings, whether in California, Texas, or New York, Carranza brings his full self. On Mother's Day during the coronavirus pandemic of 2020, Carranza took out his guitar and sang "Las Mañanitas" in Spanish to his entire administrative team, including all central leaders and superintendents, during their weekly virtual call. This honored his late mother and mirrored his consistent way of bringing his full self to the table to open the door for others to do the same.

As you lead, it is critical to open yourself up on a personal level. In an interview with Okura (2013), Brené Brown stated that bringing one's full self can also create "emotional exposure, risk, and uncertainty." But if you, as the leader, are willing to be authentic, you can expand the impact, influence, and success of your work and your life and help others do the same. It takes a lot of unnecessary energy concealing important parts of our identities—what Lahey and Kegan (2016) would say goes directly against developing a deliberately developmental organization (DDO).

Per Lahey and Kegan (2016), in the ordinary organization, nearly everyone is doing a second job no one is paying them for—namely, hiding their weaknesses, looking good, covering their rear ends, managing other people's favorable impression of them. This is the single biggest waste of a company's resources. Now imagine working in a deliberately developmental place that says, "We hired you because we thought you were *good*, not because we thought you were *perfect*." We are all here to get better, and the only way we will get better is to make mistakes, reveal our limitations, and support each other to overcome them (cited in Slocum, 2016).

Indeed, Brown emphasizes, "You can't get to courage without walking through vulnerability" (in Okura, 2013). The more willing we are to embrace vulnerability, the more courage we have to do our work the way we want to and to have the kind of impact we most desire. Consider:

- Who are you as a person?
- Who are you as a leader?
- What is your why?
- Why are you the right person to lead us?

As speaker Marianne Williamson (1996) says:

> Our deepest fear is not that we are inadequate. Our deepest fear is that we are powerful beyond measure. It is our light, not our darkness that most frightens us. We ask ourselves, Who am I to be brilliant, gorgeous, talented, fabulous? Actually, who are you *not* to be? You are a child of God. Your playing small does not serve the world. There is nothing enlightening about shrinking so that other people won't feel insecure around you. We are all meant to shine, as children do. We were born to manifest the glory of God that is within us. It's not just in some of us; it's in everyone. And as we let our own light shine, we unconsciously give other people permission to do the same. As we are liberated from our own fear, our presence automatically liberates others.

Vignette 5.2: "I never disconnected my bilingualism from my role"
Former Regional Superintendent Irma Zardoya

Puerto Rican Bronx-raised Irma Zardoya seized the opportunity to respond to New York City's call for bilingual teachers as an invitation to teach in her home borough. Throughout her career in education, she continued to give back to her home, serving as a paraprofessional, teacher, school leader, superintendent, and regional superintendent—all in the Bronx.

Being a leader in the Bronx wasn't a decision that she made explicitly. "That is where I lived and that is where I felt most comfortable. It was natural. I was born and raised in the Bronx. I got married and lived in the Bronx. My son was born in the Bronx. For a long period of time, I lived in the same complex and on the same floor with my sister in one apartment and my mother in another apartment. The Bronx is home."

In this setting, Irma brought her full self to work every single day. In 1994, she was offered the position of District 10 superintendent and had the opportunity to accept the role, in front of the entire community, in both English and Spanish. She would leverage her bilingualism consistently, even in front of the school board. And she also got together with her community often.

"We were known as the district that 'worked hard and played hard.' We used to have parties, and I would be the first one on the dance floor. The community and I would dance together. We would celebrate our heritage and music and language together."

Throughout her tenure, she stayed close to her community, whether on the dance floor or at the grocery store. Families felt valued and regularly had the opportunity to communicate in their home language. Irma never let her position as superintendent separate her from who she was as a person or from the community. The community was empowered to dream and aspire to new heights because Irma was one of them.

Viktor Frankl (1997), an Austrian neuroscientist, credited a sense of purpose and meaning with helping him survive the Holocaust: "He who has a *why* to live for can bear with almost any *how*." In order to model authenticity by leading with courage and empathy, one must have a sense of purpose. For us, that sense of purpose comes from making sure that you bring all of yourself to the table. Inspire everyone else so they can fully show up as well.

Call Out in Order to Call In

Communities that have been historically wronged will expect the same ol' same ol' and have the right to question your intentions, even if you are from the community. Welcome this initial skepticism and be intentional about how you communicate your purpose in a way that ignites heads, hearts, and hands. Your careful attention to how you are entering or reentering will help your communities feel seen, heard, and recognized for their assets versus the perceived deficits that have long defined the lens leaders carry into communities. This requires a leader to be very skilled at calling the isms out in real time while also calling people back in to invest in their growth and change. Leaders must name deficit mindsets in order to change them and own the responsibility of showing their stakeholders a path forward in service of the collective good.

For any school community to begin to create a new narrative for young people, they must first understand what deficit-based mindsets, such as the leave to succeed mindset, are and why it's important to change them. One way to build this understanding might be to ask how the L2S mindset shows up. Once the narrative is recognized in action, stakeholders can come together and begin to strategize about how to counter it. So much of communication depends on becoming a thoughtful listener, especially in communities where voices are often marginalized or silenced.

We recommend these deliberate questions:

- What are the dominant deficit-based messages getting in the way of our community's progress? Where are *we* hearing these messages? Where are *they* hearing these messages?

- Do our adults and students know how to call out deficit thinking in real time? How do we create awareness, collectively sound the alarm, and then use that data to do better?

- What process is in place to publicly identify policies and practices that perpetuate L2S behaviors and other deficit-based mindsets?

Make the dominant narratives plain enough that everyone can see their damage, and then show how they reinforce the L2S mindset. As James Baldwin wrote, "Not everything that is faced can be changed. But nothing can be changed until it is faced." You have to quickly recognize the dominant narrative—the lens through which history is told by the perspective of the dominant culture or the "invisible hand" that guides both actual reality as well as perceived reality. Dominant narratives serve the people in power, are told by the "victor," are taught as truth, and ignore multiple perspectives.

This narrative is also invisible to those within the dominant culture. As Safir (2017) says, leaders who listen "facilitate brave conversations, ask hard questions, dig into the root causes of inequity, and ensure that students, families, and colleagues from historically marginalized communities feel empowered to share their ideas and experiences." And then lift and elevate those experiences for all to learn from to decide on a clear path forward.

For example, in 2017, Jason Kamras, the 2005 National Teacher of the Year and former Obama education policy adviser, announced that his first three months as superintendent of schools in Richmond, Virginia, would focus on engaging families and the community by listening to and learning from them. To do this, Kamras held a variety of meetings with stakeholders, including neighborhood and citywide town hall meetings in all nine districts and intimate "Living Room Chats."

It is only through authentic listening that we learn to develop our "third eye" and become hyperaware of what is transpiring around us. Once they are seen, the community can get to work. It is the leader's responsibility, as the primary disrupter, to build a platform based on calling these issues to the attention of the community and tackling them one by one—creating an inclusive process to discuss the hard stuff from the onset.

Tackle Beliefs

Shifting hearts and building asset-based mindsets to redefine success requires an explicit commitment to tackle beliefs. As you tackle beliefs, it is important to ensure others are learning along with you. We do not advocate that you attempt to do it alone and be a one-person show.

Indeed, education is a problem-based field. There are numerous challenges affecting how children are educated, but how these problems are framed is a critical strategy for seeking desired improvements. Even the best leaders are not immune to applying deficit frames for solving educational issues. One belief worth tackling is accepting that every single one of us carries biases based on our lived experiences.

Indeed, growing up, we did not see a lot of explicit statements or visions of hope for Black and Brown children—whether internally or externally. Our homes were the butt of many jokes and were considered less desirable places to live, unless the neighborhood was undergoing gentrification and it was seen as a good investment by outsiders. Although amazing examples of resilient and community-centered leaders existed, we did not learn about them enough. In addition, examples of leaders who defied the L2S mindset and either stayed or returned were not commonly known or given the respect they deserve.

Examples like this appear throughout history, with many stories worth noting—people who have stepped up to change the narrative about who our communities were or who they could be. These examples exist in and out of education: Nipsey Hussle, who focused on rebuilding the Crenshaw district of South Los Angeles; Lebron James, who created a community school in his hometown of Akron, Ohio; Wendy Robinson, who returned to Fort Wayne, Indiana, as the superintendent in the halls she once walked as a kindergarten student; or Marie Izquierdo, who returned to Miami as chief academic officer, responsible for the academics of more than 350,000 students. Positive examples have always existed.

It is important for leaders to get a sense of the sociocultural and political context based on the experiences of people who either work in these settings or are served by them. Ask:

- What is your education philosophy? What do you value?
- Where do issues of race and equity play into student academic performance?
- What negative stereotypes exist about your community? What do you wish others knew about your community?

Communities like ours have had moments, though infrequent, where leaders created the space for us to speak of hope and possibilities, and for others to truly listen. In East San Jose, for example, our community has felt deep pride in the civil rights work Cesar Chavez did in our own barrio in the 1950s and 1960s. As a kid, Nancy remembers boycotting grapes ("*Uvas No!*") and picketing the Safeway parking lot. Though Chavez earned local and national recognition, leaders like Camille Llanes-Fontanilla, a Filipino American who was raised in East San Jose and for many years fearlessly led Somos Mayfair, should be equally well known and widely discussed in our schools. It is up to the leaders to create the space to share real-life stories of our community heroes and sheroes in order to shift the belief that greatness is designated to only a select few and therefore relatively unachievable.

Our communities represent what is possible when we come together to blaze a new collective trail. These moments of leadership recognition of our very own are important because they have been rare. There is an old debate about whether you start with beliefs or with practices to disrupt mindsets. Our answer: You need to tackle both, but you won't sustain practices without addressing beliefs. You will only get so far.

As Lahey and Kegan (2016) help us understand, leaders must recognize that any kind of significant culture change is an adaptive challenge that will take time. Improving outcomes for our nation's most vulnerable and most underestimated children requires deliberate and courageous leadership. The technical work required of leadership is short-lived. Disrupting deficit-based mindsets such as the L2S mindset will be messy and requires adaptive work aimed at deeply personal inner work around belief systems and bias.

Vignette 5.3: The Equity Evolution
Former Regional Superintendent Irma Zardoya

Back in my day, equity was in action as opposed to in language.

I knew I had to change systems. For example, when I first became the Bronx regional superintendent, I learned that our neediest schools were getting less in allocation than the affluent neighborhoods. Resources were literally being pushed toward affluence and giving those that had more, even more. I named it and then had everyone look at the entire allocation structure.

The big explicit and transparent goal was that everyone would get what they rightfully deserved, period. We made budgets public.

We didn't label it or have structured training, but we lived it every day in action. We also hit on other equity issues including quality instruction, special needs, facilities, bilingual education/

multilingual learners, multicultural books in schools representing our students' experiences, and access to high-quality schools.

If I knew what I knew now, we would have also been engaging
in conversations about beliefs.

So how do you tackle beliefs in real time? Lee Mun Wah (2011) would
suggest we confront them intentionally and directly by practicing high-
impact microlevel interventions:

1. Reflect back what is being said. Use their words, not yours.
2. Begin where they are, not where you want them to be.
3. Be curious and open to what they are trying to say.
4. Notice what they are saying and what they are not.
5. Emotionally relate to how they are feeling. Nurture the relationship.
6. Notice how you are feeling. Be honest and authentic. Be human.
7. Take responsibility for your part in the conflict.
8. Try to understand how their past affects who they are and how those
   experiences affect their relationship with you.
9. Stay with the process and the relationship, not just the solution.

It is also important to share a vision for what is possible. Set non-
negotiables. By 2009, after a comprehensive analysis of Miami Dade
County Schools, former superintendent Alberto Carvalho created a
strategic framework that set the unprecedented trajectory for Miami
schools. The board and superintendent leadership established expectations that would be carried out across the system; whether people liked
it or not, they knew the parameters and expectations. This approach
resulted in the school district being recognized annually as one of the
highest-performing urban school systems in the country.

Differentiate Between Investment
in Community and Investment in Ego

Partnering with the community side-by-side requires submitting your
ego to the task at hand by continuing to listen and learn. It means asking

yourself whether your decision is based on what is in your best interest or the best interest of students. Sometimes there is not a both/and proposition. Sometimes, you simply have to choose them. It means jumping in heart first, not head first. This becomes much more real when you have skin in the game.

Indeed, leaders must prioritize and promote an in-depth understanding of the community throughout their tenure. Practicing continued curiosity can come in a range of activities—from light touch to very deep touch in order to fully invest in the community you are leading. If you are from the community, you have an advantage, but you still have to do the work. There are a host of ways to invest depending on the level of investment you're willing to make. Consider the Investment/Touch Matrix shown in Figure 5.1.

Low Touch × High Investment
- **Shadow stakeholders.** Shadow students or community members in order to develop new perspectives, new narratives, and increased awareness about L2S mindsets. Marisol Rosales, in her role as the executive superintendent of Manhattan schools in New York City, made shadowing a part of her instructional rounds process across the entire borough of Manhattan during her tenure. When you shadow, let everyone know that you are not evaluating classes, educators, or the student with whom you have chosen to pair. Within minutes, you will begin to experience school in a different way than you do in your authority role. This intentional empathy can powerfully highlight opportunities to improve the conditions for learning classroom by classroom. You may wish to note

Figure 5.1 Investment/Touch Matrix

Low touch High investment	High touch High investment
Low touch Low investment	High touch Low investment

responses to these questions as important data points about the student experience:

- What are students' favorite moments in the day? What excites them?

- When do students feel the most uncomfortable or bored?

- What is the relevance of the content in classrooms to the real world?

- How are students being culturally affirmed and seen throughout the day?

- **Advocate for a public space.** Public spaces are the heart of the community. They are vibrant locations where local vendors come together, street murals are exhibited, and artists tell their stories. Is there a "neighborhood heart" in the community you are leading? In the Caribbean, there are *las plazas*; in Mexico, *zócalos* or *el parque central*; in Italy, piazzas; in New York City, public squares. At Nancy's school, a public library was placed next door to the school campus as a place where the community could gather and continue to connect.

High Touch × Low Investment

- **Go to the community.** Host meetings in the community—instead of having everyone come to you, go to them. Go to the armory or recreational center. Go to where people worship. Be thoughtful about the day of the week and time of day and potential conflicts. Consider what works better for families instead of school personnel. Announce the meetings with plenty of advance notice to allow families to plan. Offer varied sessions, virtual and in person, so that families have options.

- **Identify needs side-by-side with the community.** Consider the example from East San Jose's Somos Mayfair where visitors immerse themselves into the neighborhood through a walking tour to learn about the struggle and history of the community as well as continued needs. Visitors then debrief side-by-side with community members to strengthen partnerships and identify entry points to address the needs noted during their walking tour.

- **Conduct a neighborhood walk.** Stroll through the community surrounding the school. Get to know the local bodegas, *panaderías*, parks, playgrounds, places of worship, community centers, and the like. Through community walks around students' neighborhoods, educators and school staff can learn from those they teach, creating a stronger and more responsive school community.

  Shane Safir (2017a), founding principal of the June Jordan School for Equity in San Francisco, shares this advice in planning for a community walk:

  1. **Set a clear purpose.** Why has our school or team chosen to do community walks? Which community do we hope to learn more about?
  2. **Craft a learning question.** Can you clearly state what you wonder about or hope to learn from this experience?
  3. **Create norms to promote respect.** Have you and your staff discussed how to model respect as you enter the community? Have you created norms to guide faculty behavior?
  4. **Invite students, families, and the community to participate.** Have you asked parents and students to identify the most important places for teachers to visit and learn about? Have you coached students to design an engaging experience? Have you organized a meeting with leaders from the community you will visit?
  5. **Structure the experience.** Have you created time during the workday for staff to participate? Have you built in time (at least an hour) for a thorough debrief of the experience? Have you planned a reflection process for staff to share key learnings? (para. 9)

High Touch × High Investment

- **Become a volunteer.** Volunteerism builds rapport and community wealth and is an investment in love. Serving the community is a clear sign of commitment. Be of service.

- **Make home visits a common practice.** Engage in the home visitation process to ensure that every single student and family is connected to an adult at the school. Mapp et al. (2017) argue for home visits as a critical method for gathering explicit and important knowledge about the child and the community. And don't just visit once—make it part of your regular practice. We offer these questions as an initial prompt:

- Tell me about your family.
- From your perspective, what are your child's strengths?
- What are your child's challenges?
- What are the most important things to you regarding your child's education?
- What do you need from me?

- **Live with host families.** In 2009, Chicago launched STEP-UP (Summer Teacher Education Partnership for Urban Preparation) to create a pathway for full immersion for new teachers. This sort of initiative is not a common approach to teacher-community engagement because the ability to engage in a full-immersion program might not be feasible. However, this doesn't mean leaders cannot encourage ongoing dialogues between teachers and the students and families they serve. STEP-UP reports that more than 80 percent of fellows are still in the classroom in Chicago or other high-needs areas beyond the five-year mark, which is unlike the national average (Friedman, 2015).

- **Move to/live in the community.** If you want to invest in and truly understand what it means to lead in your community, live there. This move will build trust for you as the leader, knowing that this is not merely a job but that you are one with the community, as a learner and resident of the community.

- **Send your own kids to the school system you lead.** This is the ultimate investment—have your own children attend the schools you are leading. As a school principal, Nancy remembers board members and superintendents who would get on their soapbox and tell us what to do or what not to do to improve the lives of "those kids" but never had skin in the game. Instead, many of them sent their kids to private schools in a different neighborhood.

True, there are advantages to leaders who know their communities well. The findings of a study on homegrown rural school leaders reveal that prior history and relationships within the district and community, as well as the deep understanding and background knowledge they have of the values and culture of the district and community, allow leaders to have an easier time building and maintaining trust and relationships, creating a positive school culture, and enacting change. Additionally, their deep understanding of the challenges have given them foresight to help them better understand and manage specific dilemmas in their districts.

In most rural and suburban schools, students are taught by teachers who have similar experiences to themselves. Many of these teachers went to the same or similar schools, live in the same communities, and hail from comparable socioeconomic backgrounds. But that's not often the case when it comes to urban communities. Therefore, it is important to continue practicing curiosity and learning throughout your tenure. It never ends.

The guiding north star is active participation. United Nations secretary-general Kofi Annan (2001) stressed that "no society can claim to be based on justice and equality without [affected persons] making decisions as full-fledged members."

The skill of practicing and modeling curiosity by continuing to learn is key. As writer Ken Blanchard says, "No one of us is as smart as all of us together." The question then becomes about how deeply you as the leader want to invest—how will you model this and encourage your staff to do the same?—and whether you've chosen the work and the community over your ego.

Lead from Behind the Eyes

Enacting a culture of pride in identity and community through food, fun, and fiesta is not enough. That work is superficial, and leaders must be ready to dive in and do the work required. Consider this unforgettable line in *To Kill a Mockingbird*, where Atticus Finch posits, "If you just learn a single trick, Scout, you'll get along a lot better with all kinds of folks. You never really understand a person until you consider things from his point of view . . . until you climb inside of his skin and walk around in it" (Lee, 2006).

There is no greater activity to learn about each other's needs than immersing oneself into each other's experience. The horrific death of George Floyd in 2020 compelled Tawanna Grover, former superintendent of Grand Island Public Schools in Nebraska, to share how this tragic event affected her as a person and as a district leader. She shared with the community, "I am a black woman and mother of two black men, and a leader of a diverse school district. When the video of Mr. Floyd lying under the knee of a police officer went viral, all I could see were my sons, my brother, and my students in his pleading, terrified face." She recognized that we must "lift as we lead" (Grover, 2020, para. 2).

Grover reminds us that unrest can bind us all together. She is a servant leader who provides thousands of students and employees with a vision for excellence. To fully understand all facets of the school organization, she often spends a day-in-the-life of her staff members to better understand what is working as well as where improvements can be made. For instance, she would spend the day as a cafeteria worker, a behavioral coach, an attendance caller, and a construction worker on site, and she has spent time in a gifted and talented class. Grover learned, for example, that some of the cafeteria workers regularly went into their own pockets to help students pay for lunches. As she always tells people, she is a better leader because she knows how to "change shoes."

As an educator, ethnographer, and leader, you're putting yourself in the shoes of another.

The majority of teachers entering the profession don't necessarily come from or deeply understand the diverse cultures and communities in which they will teach. This is particularly true in minority-majority schools. Schools must take steps to ensure their educators are equipped with the knowledge, skills, strategies, and attitudes necessary to work effectively with students from diverse backgrounds and their families (Stachowski & Mahan, 2001).

At the beginning of each school year in Memphis, Tennessee, Bobby White, founder and CEO of Frayser Community Schools, organizes a neighborhood tour for Frayser faculty and staff. Since they all live outside the school community, Bobby knows he has to center them in the community's DNA. He secures the buses, and students serve as tour guides.

The students are proud to show off where they live, where they attend religious services, and where their families buy groceries. This engagement has proven so successful that additional tours have been organized for school partners, funders, religious leaders, businessmen, and elected officials. These annual tours bring to life the richness of North Memphis and Frayser. White believes that if you are committed to Frayer students, then you must appreciate the greatness of where they come from.

The idea of getting behind the eyes is not new. A study of Native American tribal leaders in California revealed that the way a community tells its stories matters, as seeing communities through its strengths helped to counter its dominant, common trauma narratives and helped to build psychological resilience. "As leaders of a federally unrecognized tribal group, they adopted a narrative of 'survivance,' which appears to buffer psychosocial stress and provide a resilient narrative identity" (Vizenor, 2008). This term *survivance* combines the terms *survival* and *resistance* to assert that, for Indigenous people and many others from historically marginalized groups, survival has required resistance. "Survivance is an example of a collective narrative identity engagement utilized by indigenous peoples to reframe identity discourses beyond colonial trappings of erasure and victimhood."

When we as leaders work to get behind the eyes, especially of groups that have been minoritized, we begin to understand their experience and value their "survivance" identities. We must build upon our strengths and the enduring capacity for resilience as people who have survived racism and oppression. Indeed, stories that reflect a community's strengths create a resilient mindset.

It is important that our youth do not feel like they need to be someone different in your school community to experience success. In his work on code switching, Emdin (2016) argues that a distinction must be made between the skill of code switching and teaching students to be unnaturally like others for acceptance. "When one becomes trained to be someone other than who they are, they become disingenuous or inauthentic." Emdin argues that supporting students creates a hybridized identity that allows them to bring their true selves while expressing and navigating multiple cultures with multiple codes. Otherwise, students are inadvertently encouraged to separate themselves from their identities in order to "'make it out of the hood' rather than celebrate what their histories, neighborhoods, and home communities have to offer" (p. 177).

As you get behind the eyes, make it a point to learn the history of the community as well as various points of data and information (well beyond test scores). Research these questions:

- What stories do people tell about their experiences?
- What and who is valued in this community, and how do we all know?
- What are the shallow manifestations of food, fun, and fiesta in this community? What would it take to go deeper and really make our students feel seen, respected, and heard?
- Who is included in this community, and who is not?
- Where and how do I need to get behind the eyes to deeply understand the community's needs?

Getting behind the eyes allows for a leader to truly understand the values that undergird the refined definition of success because they are able to see, in plain view, the tremendous assets the community brings to the table.

Activate the Counternarrative

There is no question that the public-facing stories that are told about many communities—especially those where the majority of residents are people of color—are stories of loss, tragedy, crime, and hopelessness. Simply turn on the news to see this deficit-based framing and portrayal for yourself. Sadly, this isn't new.

No matter what those narratives are, though, there are counternarratives to those stories in every place, and young people in these communities yearn to be able to hear and tell the other truths of the places they call home.

In a community called Back of the Yards in Chicago, the 3rd grade students of Chavez Elementary School took this personally. Frustrated by the stories they frequently heard on the news about their neighborhood, they decided they would create an outlet to share their own version of the news. They created an online magazine called *Dilo Fuerte,* or "Say It Loud." Working with their teachers, Ashley McCall and Lindsay

Singer, they wrote stories highlighting the positive things happening in their community under the hashtag #myhoodmyheadline. The magazine includes interviews with neighborhood residents, poetry, and more (Kelleher, 2019). In 2020, the "Say Their Names" education toolkit gained traction in school districts across the country to talk about racial violence with kids (myips.org). Intended to provide tools and resources, it included a segment on "How is the story being told, and why is that important?"

However, rumors, misinformation, and blatant lies about our homes stubbornly persist. Efforts to justify atrocious acts against people of color are often told through deficit-based narratives, suggesting that a Black man like George Floyd was a criminal, that Trayvon Martin was up to no good, that Ahmaud Arbery looked suspicious as he jogged through a white neighborhood. Similarly, educators are often led to believe that students of color in low-income communities are "ghetto" or don't care about school or their own success. Nor do their parents, they say. We saw this point depicted clearly with the tragic loss of 13-year-old Adam Toledo of Chicago's Little Village. Such justifications usually go like this: "If they [people of color] were not out that late, they would still be alive. If they [people of color] would just comply with law enforcement, they would still be alive."

As frustrating as these narratives are to hear, leaders do not do enough to counter them, both inside and outside the school building. For example, why didn't it become a mainstream conversation that George Floyd dreamed of being a Supreme Court justice as a 2nd grader, that friends called him the "Big Friendly," or that he was a star athlete with the potential to play professionally? Why didn't we talk about the fact that 17-year-old Trayvon Martin was a kind-hearted kid who was one of the best players on the Wolverines, his recreational football team in Miramar, Florida? Or that Trayvon's dad would attend every game and leverage football as a way to keep his son focused? Or that Ahmaud Arbery, known as "Maud," was a humble person and a high school football standout and that 13-year-old Adam Toledo was a talented artist?

These counternarratives are consistently left out of the conversations, and storytelling becomes a one-way street in communities of color. Turning victims into villains, they require an active dismantling of those stories and offerings of counternarratives. However, the narrative cannot shift in the absence of active work by leaders across our communities—and when leaders own and recite counternarratives, they provide the language needed for their stakeholders to do the same.

This is true in society and in our schools—we often label our students of color living in low-income communities as failures before they even arrive on scene. We serve young people best when we create spaces for and encourage them to tell stories of power, optimism, opportunity, strength, and joy. We need to build up communities rather than tear them down and acknowledge the complexities of their journeys the way we would want someone to honor ours.

There are three considerations in thinking about storytelling as we lead to change the narrative in order to redefine success and apply an asset-based frame to every decision we make:

- What stories we tell about the communities we serve.
- How we create the opportunities for communities to share their stories of strength, hope, and possibility with the staff that serve them.
- What structures we have put in place to actively counter the dominant narratives told about our communities.

As 2019 Louisiana State Superintendent of the Year T. Lamar Goree shares, "As educators, we ask our students to explore their wildest dreams. In doing so, we ask them to see no barriers. While this is wonderful, it also creates the belief that those barriers push students outside of their home area in order to become who they are supposed to be. As a community, it is our shared obligation to provide access to training and careers that allow children to explore their greatest horizons right in their own backyard."

Telling a new set of stories also begins with rewriting the narratives we tell about our own communities and the communities we serve, whether those are one and the same or not. What if, as educators, we could drive the shift in those deficit-based narratives? What if, in every interaction, we could tell the stories of the strengths of the communities we serve? And what if, especially, we could constantly communicate a narrative of strength and beauty to the students themselves?

There is power in these narratives. By telling stories of assets and opportunities, we help young people see themselves as part of their communities and already made up of everything they need to be successful in life. And we help others see the beauty in every community and commit to ensuring that everyone has what they need and deserve. Most important, we protect the dignity of each individual, and we hold one another accountable, rather than expecting our young people to escape from the spaces we have created for them.

If you, as an educator, have ever described to an outsider the level of poverty or crime in the community you serve, you have been guilty of creating a deficit-based narrative about that community. Well-intentioned or not, this kind of narrative only serves to alienate people from the community and to reinforce stereotypes and implicit biases about people and places. Ask these questions instead:

- What makes your community special?
- What are the strengths and values of the people?
- What does the community do better than anyone else?
- Who are the artists, doctors, and inventors from your community?
- What is the history of the place?
- What plants grow best in the region?

As our colleague Katiusca Moreno, a former student of Marshall Ganz and a leader in education, often says, "If you do not tell your own story, someone else will."

Forging a New Model for Leadership

So what does leadership have to do with redefining success, and for whom?

Well, success for kids, similar to adults, follows a set of unspoken rules within the dominant culture. Successful leaders look like this, speak like this, dress like this. These are the things that work; these are the things that don't work. There is a playbook marinated in dominant and traditional practices that keep our leaders, especially our leaders of color, at bay and confined. These silent rules can limit the freedom of a leader to lead in ways that help communities connect and dream together. They also unconsciously perpetuate student outcomes in communities of color that don't lift and elevate the potential of our communities that need it most.

It is always easy to blame kids and communities, but leaders must own the change, and it will require going out on a limb in order to truly redefine success from an asset-based frame. Leaders have the opportunity and challenge to dispel stereotypes about the communities they serve by offering models of how it is done.

- **Model authenticity:** When I bring my full self to the table, my students, families, and teachers will bring their full selves too.

- **Call out in order to call in:** When I call out deep-seated problems and inequities from a problem-solving perspective, I open the door for others to name the thing they've been hesitant to name for some time. It is only then that we can work to rebuild.

- **Tackle beliefs:** When I am willing to engage in public and private conversations about how my own lived experiences color my lens and perspective, I free others to be vulnerable and share. It is only then that we, as a community, can have honest conversations about deep-seated beliefs.

- **Differentiate between investment in community and investment in ego:** When I catch my ego getting in the way and name that publicly, I open the door to true growth, change, and continuous learning.

- **Lead from behind the eyes:** When I take a moment to step into the shoes and experiences of others, they will get behind mine, too, and together we can offer grace as we learn and grow together.

- **Activate the counternarrative:** When I actively share asset-based stories and the beauty of our community outwardly, I create space for others to reframe the harmful dominant narratives that have plagued our communities for centuries.

These six moves defy much of what the dominant narrative tells you your job is and should be. Indeed, we need to hold the mirror up to ourselves to do something different to redefine what it means for a leader and communities to be successful. This has a cascading effect.

As Meisha Ross Porter, president of the Bronx Community Foundation, has stated, "I don't want my leadership to be inaccessible and separate from who I am as a person. I want my community members to bump into me in the long line at Target or the bodega down the block. Our community needs to see me, as the city's former chancellor, living lives like them. Struggling with the same issues including my own policies about schools because my kids are in the system." Ross Porter reminds us that it is a leader's responsibility to create pathways for stakeholders to see themselves in our leaders. When she was a principal, she joked that her oldest daughter would protest at the supermarket when they saw families shopping there: "Mom, please, you're not the principal of the supermarket." Ross Porter would respond, "I am the principal of everywhere."

The six leadership moves are reminders of humanity, agency, and ways to offer power to the "powerless" and voice to the "voiceless." This is not an if/then proposition; it is a set of suggested steps we have seen work well to forge a new path of leadership for leaders themselves, those who follow them, and all stakeholders who engage in a newer, more inclusive form of leadership.

SHOULDER UP

1. How does a leader proactively redefine success? Explore where your notions of success derive from and where they show up in your leadership. What steps can you take to inspire a new way of thinking? Call a leader you respect and admire. Ask them what success in their leadership looks and sounds like, paying close attention to the evidence they collect to know if they are successful.

2. Do you believe change happens through practices or beliefs? What has worked? What hasn't? What are your next steps? What is your entry point with your stakeholders, and how do you know? What does that mean for your leadership? Engage in this debate with others in your context. Use the information you collect to keep learning.

3. What do you need to stop, start, or continue doing in your leadership? Acknowledge the fact that as a leader, you likely perpetuate deficit-based mindsets such as the leave to succeed mindset. What do you need to change about your notions of what it means to be an effective leader or student? What mental models do you need to shift, and how will you unlearn what, within your practice, isn't working for your community?

Acknowledgments

Roberto: To God Be the Glory

Pa mi familia: Thank you for being my inspiration. I am reminded daily of the edict "To whom much has been given, much is expected" because of my responsibility to help make the world a better place. You have taught me to live in the moment, focus on getting 1 percent better each day, and that serving and loving others are the greatest honors.

To my loved ones who are not biological but might as well be: *pa lante, we got this. Dale!*

To the SuptBourbon Group: Our Friday sessions during COVID and our fellowship were desperately needed. Thank you for the positive, empowering memories in Ithaca and beyond.

I am New York born, Newburgh bred, and Bronx strong. *Soy Boricua pa' que tu lo sepa.*

La Nancy

Pa mi familia: to my abuelita Sol, you sacrificed everything for us. None of this is possible without you. For Maria del Socorro Escobedo Gutiérrez—my mother and my greatest teacher. I live in your grace and I am humbled by your story. Thank you for blessing me with five best friends—my beautiful brothers and sisters. Thank you for reminding us through your actions that we are responsible for solving the problems in our own backyard.

To my loves, Chris and Kaicifo: In Lak'ech. I am because you are. *Los quiero mucho.* To the Leadership Academy: Thank you for seeing and accepting all of me. To Salez, EdLD, Pahara 2gether4ever—I love you. And for East San Jose—the most beautiful community I've ever known. Let this shine as an example of our potential—the potential schools have the responsibility to nurture and develop, and never doubt. Our struggle is our motivation. Our resilience is our strength. This is for us.

Together: Nosotros

To the amazing person who introduced us to each other in 2010—our mentor and shero, Deborah Jewell-Sherman: It's an honor to be your chareb. You have always loved and supported us as familia. Thank you for writing such a beautiful foreword.

To the homies—Los Criticos: Meisha Ross Porter, Carlos Moreno, and Karen Maldonado: We love you and are thankful for your support. Our leadership journeys have more memories to come.

To NYSALAS/ALAS: We stand on the shoulders of giants. Gracias for having our backs. #Cohort3

Writing a book is an overwhelming task. We want to give a heartfelt shout-out to our writing partners and supporters: Colin Seale, Shanna Peeples, Tina Owen-Moore, and Jill Grossman.

References

Adichie, N. C. (2009). The danger of a single story. Ted Global 2009. https://www.ted
    .com/talks/chimamanda_ngozi_adichie_the_danger_of_a_single_story
Andrade, J. (2002). Note to educators: Hope required when growing roses in
    concrete. *Harvard Educational Review.*
Annan, K. (2001). *Nobel lecture delivered by Kofi Annan.* United Nations. https://
    www.un.org/sg/en/content/sg/speeches/2001-12-10/nobel-lecture-delivered
    -kofi-annan
Anti-Displacement Policy Network (ADPN). (2020). *Ending displacement in
    San Jose: Community Strategy Repor*t. https://www.sanjoseca.gov/home
    /showdocument?id=50333
Bell, L. A., Rosemarie A. R., Kayhan I., & Brett, M. (2008). Learning about race and
    racism through storytelling and the arts. Storytelling Project, Barnard College.
    http://www.columbia.edu/itc/barnard/education/stp/stp_curriculum.pdf
Blakemore E. (2022, January 11). How dolls helped win *Brown v. Board of Education*:
    Deceptively simple doll tests helped the Supreme Court to strike down school
    segregation. https://history.com/news/brown-v-board-of-education-doll
    -experiment
Boozer, L., Kelley, L., Peterkin, R., & Sherman, D. (2011). *Every child, every classroom,
    every day: School leaders who are making equity a reality.* Wiley.
Boyle, G. (2010). *Tattoos on the heart: The power of boundless compassion.* Free Press.
Cepada, E. J. (2013, August 10). In education, a "probrecito" syndrome. *Salt Lake
    Tribune.* https://archive.sltrib.com/article.php?id=56717963&itype=CMSID
Chenoweth, K. (2021). *Districts that succeed: Breaking the correlation between race,
    poverty, and achievement.* Harvard Education Press.
City, E. A., Elmore, R. F., Fiarman, S. E., & Teitel, L. (2009). *Instructional rounds in
    education: A network approach to improving teaching and learning.* Harvard
    University Press.
Delpit, L. (2006). *Other people's children: Cultural conflict in the classroom.* New
    Press.
Du Bois, W. E. B. (1935). Does the Negro need separate schools? *The Journal of
    Negro Education, 4*(3), pp. 328–335.
DuFour, R. (2004). What is a professional learning community? *Educational
    Leadership.*
Dweck, C. S. (2008). *Mindset: The new psychology of success.* New York: Ballantine
    Books.
Emdin, C. (2016). *For white folks who teach in the hood . . . and the rest of y'all too:
    Reality pedagogy and urban education.* Beacon.

Frank, A. (2019). Rapper Nipsey Hussle's death put an inspiring life in the spotlight. https://www.vox.com/culture/2019/4/2/18290487/nipsey-hussle-death-rapper

Frankl, V. (1997). Viktor Frankl Institut. https://www.univie.ac.at/logotherapy/lifeandwork.html

Friedman, B. (2015, July 20). Education: Student teachers "STEP-UP" to Chicago. WTTW News. https://news.wttw.com/2015/07/20/student-teachers-step-chicago

Ganz, M. (2012). Public narrative, collective action, and power. *Harvard Business Review*.

Gardner, H. (1983). *Frames of mind: The theory of multiple intelligences*. Basic Books.

Gonzalez, A. (2019). Hispanics with darker skin are more likely to experience discrimination than those with lighter skin. Pew Research Center. https://www.pewresearch.org/fact-tank/2019/07/02/hispanics-with-darker-skin-are-more-likely-to-experience-discrimination-than-those-with-lighter-skin/

Grissom, J., Egalite, A., & Lind, C. (2021). *How principals affect students and schools: A systematic synthesis of two decades of research*. Wallace Foundation.

Grover, T. (2020). GI superintendent: I am also a black woman and the mother of two black men. https://www.1011now.com/content/news/GI-Superintendent---571168051.html

Hammond, Z. L. (2015). *Culturally responsive teaching and the brain: Promoting authentic engagement and rigor among culturally and linguistically diverse students*. Corwin.

Herrnstein, R. J., & Murray, C. A. (1994). *The bell curve: Intelligence and class structure in American life*. Free Press.

Horsford, S. (2011). *Learning in a burning house: Educational inequality, ideology, and (dis)integration*. Teachers College Press.

Joshi Hansen, U. (2017, November 28). The future of smart. TEDx Crestmoor Park Women. https://www.youtube.com/watch?v=MxAwul1P6xQ

Kelleher, M. (2019, July 8). When it comes to pride in their neighborhood, third graders at Chavez elementary say it loud. Chicago Unheard. https://chicagounheard.org/blog/when-it-comes-to-pride-in-their-neighborhood-third-graders-at-chavez-elementary-say-it-loud

King, M. (1967). *Where do we go from here: Chaos or community?* Harper & Row.

Kirwan Institute. (2018). Implicit bias module series. Ohio State University. http://kirwaninstitute.osu.edu/implicit-bias-training/

Lahey, L., & Kegan, R. (2016). *An everyone culture: Becoming a deliberately developmental organization*. Harvard Business Review Press.

Lee, H. (2006). *To kill a mockingbird*. Harper Perennial Modern Classics.

Leithwood, K., Louis, K. S., Anderson, S., & Wahlstrom, K. (2004). *How leadership influences student learning*. The Wallace Foundation. https://www.wallacefoundation.org/knowledge-center/pages/how-leadership-influences-student-learning.aspx

Leithwood et al. (2010). *Investigating the links to improved student learning: Final report of research findings*. The Wallace Foundation. https://conservancy.umn.edu/bitstream/handle/11299/140885/Learning-from-Leadership_Final-Research-Report_July-2010.pdf?sequence=1&isAllowed=y

Lopez, N. (2019). East San Jose leaders discuss how housing crisis impacts Latino community. *East San Jose Spotlight*. https://sanjosespotlight.com/east-san-jose-leaders-discuss-how-housing-crisis-impacts-latino-community/

Mapp, K., Carver, I., & Lander, J. (2017). *Powerful partnerships: A teacher's guide to engaging families for student success*. Scholastic.

Mascareñaz, L. (2008, November 30). Why Susana Cordova is the right pick to lead Denver's schools into the next chapter. *The 74*. https://www.the74million.org /article/mascarenaz-cordova-can-lead-denver-into-the-next-chapter/

Masterson, M. (2021, September 29). Janice Jackson named CEO of HOPE Chicago, nonprofit seeking to provide $1B in scholarships. WTTW News. https://news .wttw.com/2021/09/29/janice-jackson-named-ceo-hope-chicago-nonprofit -seeking-provide-1b-scholarships

McDonald, V. (2017). *Demanding their rights: The Latino struggle for educational access and equity*. Council of Parent Attorneys and Advocates. https://cdn .ymaws.com/www.copaa.org/resource/resmgr/SREC_Files/Latino /Demanding_their_Rights_The_L.pdf

Mehta, J., & Fine, S. M. (2019). *In search of deeper learning: The quest to remake the American high school*. Harvard University Press.

Meier, D. (2013, April 11). Explaining KIPP's "SLANT." *Education Week*.

Muhammad, G. E. (2020). *Cultivating genius: An equity framework for culturally and historically responsive literacy*. Scholastic Teaching Resources.

Mun Wah, L. (2021). StirFry Seminars. https://stirfryseminars.com/about-stirfry /lee-mun-wah/

Okura, L. (2013, September 12). Brené Brown: "You can't get to courage without walking through vulnerability." *Huffington Post*.

Oluo, I. (2018). *So you want to talk about race*. Seal.

Padilla, R. (2019). Courageous conversations, concrete Actions. *School Administrator*.

Patterns for Progress. (2016). TK

Pizarro, M. (2014). Baraka wins mayoral contest in Newark. *Observer*. https:// observer.com/2014/05/breaking-baraka-wins-mayoral-contest-in-newark/

Ramírez, A. M., Morales, V. J. G., & Rojas, R. M. (2011). Knowledge creation, organizational learning and their effects on organizational performance. *Engineering Economics, 22*(3), 309–318.

Reed, A. (2021, March 24). Nipsey Hussle remembered: New biography of late rapper is as celebratory as it is heartbreaking. *USA Today*. https://www.usatoday.com /story/entertainment/books/2021/03/24/nipsey-hussle-new-book-rob -kenner-marathon-dont-stop/4801695001/

Robinson, D. (2020). Stop with racist history: A global call to teach African history. https://link.medium.com/SY9aoNVQIlb

Safir, S. (2017a, March 23). Community walks create bonds of understanding. *Edutopia*. https://www.edutopia.org/blog/community-walks-create-bonds -understanding-shane-safir

Safir, S. (2017b). *The listening leader: Creating the conditions for equitable school transformation*. Wiley.

Santelises, S. (2020, May 11). Baltimore schools CEO: We will not hold low-income students back a grade because of coronavirus. *Baltimore Sun*. https://www .baltimoresun.com/opinion/op-ed/bs-ed-op-0512-sonja-santelesis -coronavirus-20200511-a526qjulvfhxpb32x4pfucjn6m-story.html

Santelises, S. (2021). Baltimore Public Schools: Meet the CEO. https://www .baltimorecityschools.org/ceo-sonja-santelises

Seale, C. (2018). Here's the one thing you haven't heard about LeBron's new school. *Ed Post*. https://www.edpost.com/stories/heres-the-one-thing-you-havent -heard-about-lebrons-new-school

Seale, C. (2020). *Thinking like a lawyer: A framework for teaching critical thinking to all students*. Prufrock.

Singleton, G. (2014). *Courageous conversations about race: A field guide for achieving equity in schools* (2nd ed.). Corwin.

Slocum, D. (2016). *5 questions with Robert Kegan, Lisa Lahey and Andy Fleming: On "An Everyone Culture."* Berlin School of Creative Leadership.

Stachowski, L., & Mahan, J. (2001). *Cross-cultural field placements: Student teachers learning from schools and communities.* University of Nebraska Press.

Sue, D. (2010, November). Microaggressions: More than just race. *Psychology Today.* https://www.psychologytoday.com/us/blog/microaggressions-in-everyday-life/201011/microaggressions-more-just-race

Sue, D. (2015). *Race talk and the conspiracy of silence: Understanding and facilitating difficult dialogues on race.* Wiley.

Tatum, B. (2003). *Why are all the black kids sitting together in the cafeteria?* Basic Books.

TNTP. (2018). *The Opportunity Myth: What students can show us about how school is letting them down and how to fix it.* https://tntp.org/publications/view/the-opportunity-myth

TNTP. (2021). *Accelerate, don't remediate: New evidence from elementary math classrooms.* https://tntp.org/publications/view/teacher-training-and-classroom-practice/acc

Valenzuela, A. (1999). *Subtractive schooling: U.S. and Mexican youth and the politics of caring.* State University of New York Press.

Vera, A., & Hayes, M. (2020). Graduate together: Honoring the class of 2020. CNN. https://www.cnn.com/us/live-news/graduate-together-2020/index.html

Vizenor, G. R. (2008). *Survivance: Narratives of Native presence.* University of Nebraska Press.

Williamson, M. (1996). *A return to love: Reflections on the principles of a course in miracles.* HarperOne.

Woodson, C. (2016). *The mis-education of the Negro.* Africa World Press. (Originally published 1933)

Yin, A. (2017, September 8). Education by the numbers. *New York Times.* https://www.nytimes.com/2017/09/08/magazine/education-by-the-numbers.html

Index

The letter *f* following a page number denotes a figure.

About the Authors

 **Dr. Nancy B. Gutiérrez** is president and CEO of The Leadership Academy, a nationally recognized nonprofit organization dedicated to supporting and developing school and school system leaders to dismantle inequities in schools and create the conditions necessary for all students to thrive. Since 2003, The Leadership Academy has worked with educators in more than 200 school districts, state education departments, and education organizations across 37 states; Washington, DC; and internationally.

Nancy joined The Leadership Academy in 2014 and has served as National Leadership Designer and Facilitator, Vice President of District Leadership, and Chief Strategy Officer. She was named President and CEO in October 2018. She is a Fall 2019 Pahara-Aspen Education Fellow and was named one of the top 100 most influential leaders in education in New York in 2020. In 2023, Nancy was name San Jose State University's Distinguished Alumna. Nancy is a frequent keynote speaker for local and national education organizations and has authored numerous pieces on education leadership and equity for national publications including *Education Week, Kappan, The74*, Learning Forward's *Learning Professional, District Administrator*, and *Hechinger Report.*

Nancy began her career as a teacher and principal in her home community of East San Jose, California, where she was the founding principal of Renaissance Academy, the highest-performing middle school in the district and a California Distinguished School. She also led the successful effort to turn around the district's lowest-performing middle school. She was named the UC-Davis Rising Star and Association of California

School Administrators' Region 8 Middle School Principal of the Year in 2010. Prior to her tenure with the Leadership Academy, Nancy launched a program for executive leadership advancement for the New York City Department of Education that led to superintendent certification.

Nancy is a graduate of the inaugural cohort of the Harvard Graduate School of Education's Doctor of Education Leadership (Ed.L.D.) program and is a graduate of the Association of Latino Administrators and Superintendents (ALAS) Aspiring Superintendents Academy. She served on the national board of the Coalition of Essential Schools for more than a decade. She is an instructor at NYU and frequently teaches at the Harvard Principals' Center institutes for School Turnaround Leaders, Urban School Leaders, and Race, Equity, Access, and Leadership. Nancy is a member of the board of directors at the Hunt Institute, brightbeam, and Education Leaders of Color (EdLoC) and serves on the Latinos for Education teaching team.

Dr. Roberto Padilla is the superintendent of Community School District 7 in the Bronx. From humble beginnings as a child, Roberto learned early on in his life the true meaning of resiliency and grit. He is a life-long educator, having been a teacher, assistant principal, principal, executive coach, and leadership consultant. Even today, he considers himself a teacher who just happens to be a superintendent.

Prior to becoming a superintendent, Roberto was a teacher and principal in New York City. He is widely recognized for his leadership in turning around failing schools and supporting school district leaders on change leadership. He considers himself to be an equity warrior whose purpose is to give all children a fighting chance at having a productive life. He is committed to placing effective teachers and school leaders in every school.

Roberto was recognized as the 2021 New York State (NYS) Superintendent of the Year, a 2021 National Trio Achiever, and the 2019 Education Week Leader to Learn From. These are prestigious national recognitions that reflect his commitment to districtwide equity and excellence. As part of his training, Roberto was a fellow for the Broad

Center at Yale School of Management, a Deeper Learning Equity Fellow, and an Education Policy Fellow at Columbia University, and he served a four-year term as a board member for Harvard University's Principal Center. He received his doctorate from Fordham University.

Roberto is the founding president of the NYS Association of Latino Administrators and Superintendents, serves as an executive member of the NYS Council of School Superintendents, and is a former trustee of the Montefiore Cornwall St. Luke's Hospital. He is a graduate of the AASA National Superintendents Program and the Association of Latino Administrators and Superintendents (ALAS) Superintendent Leadership Academy (SLA). He is a published author, has presented at national conferences, serves as an executive coach, and sits on many nonprofit boards.

Related ASCD Resources

At the time of publication, the following resources were available (ASCD stock numbers in parentheses).

Cultivating Joyful Learning Spaces for Black Girls: Insights into Interrupting School Pushout by Monique W. Morris (Monique Couvson) (#121004)

Five Practices for Equity-Focused School Leadership by Sharon I. Radd, Gretchen Givens Generett, Mark Anthony Gooden, and George Theoharis (#120008)

Fix Injustice, Not Kids and Other Principles for Transformative Equity Leadership by Paul Gorski and Katy Swalwell (#120012)

The Innocent Classroom: Dismantling Racial Bias to Support Students of Color by Alexs Pate (#120025)

Leading Within Systems of Inequity in Education: A Liberation Guide for Leaders of Color by Mary Rice-Boothe (#123014)

Leading Your School Toward Equity: A Practical Framework for Walking the Talk by Dwayne Chism (#123003)

The Power of Place: Authentic Learning Through Place-Based Education by Tom Vander Ark, Emily Liebtag, and Nate McClennen (#120017)

For up-to-date information about ASCD resources, go to www.ascd.org. You can search the complete archives of *Educational Leadership* at www.ascd.org/el. To contact us, send an email to member@ascd.org or call 1-800-933-2723 or 703-578-9600.

WHOLE CHILD
TENETS

The ASCD Whole Child approach is an effort to transition from a focus on narrowly defined academic achievement to one that promotes the long-term development and success of all children. Through this approach, ASCD supports educators, families, community members, and policymakers as they move from a vision about educating the whole child to sustainable, collaborative actions.

Stay and Prevail relates to the **safe, engaged,** and **supported** tenets.

For more about the ASCD Whole Child approach, visit **www.ascd.org/wholechild.**

1 HEALTHY
Each student enters school healthy and learns about and practices a healthy lifestyle.

2 SAFE
Each student learns in an environment that is physically and emotionally safe for students and adults.

3 ENGAGED
Each student is actively engaged in learning and is connected to the school and broader community.

4 SUPPORTED
Each student has access to personalized learning and is supported by qualified, caring adults.

5 CHALLENGED
Each student is challenged academically and prepared for success in college or further study and for employment and participation in a global environment.